A Key to the Destiny of Man

This exciting selection from the writings of outstanding Greek historians explores many of the far-reaching ideas and ideals of their civilization. Brilliantly translated by the eminent historian, Arnold J. Toynbee, author of the monumental *A Study of History,* the book offers a rewarding look at those experiences of the ancients that may give us a key to the riddle of our own destiny. It is Toynbee's strong belief, first expressed in an earlier volume, *Greek Historical Thought,* that there is a close parallel between Hellenic civilization and our own, and that the problems which confront us today are analogous to many of those faced by the Greek world.

Following Toynbee's illuminating introduction, generous selections from Herodotus, Polybius, Xenophon and others, deal with such aspects of Greek civilization as the problem of class warfare, the rules of war, relations between the Greeks and the barbarians, etc. One of the most important passages is Thucydides' penetrating analysis of power politics, the dialogue dealing with the revolt of Melos against Athens in 416 B.C.

An invaluable introduction to the history of the ancient world, this fascinating book is also a stimulating and thought-provoking reading experience.

THIS BOOK IS A REPRINT OF THE ORIGINAL HARD-COVER EDITION, PUBLISHED BY THE BEACON PRESS

Other MENTOR Books of Interest

Greek Civilization and Character

THE SELF-REVELATION OF ANCIENT GREEK SOCIETY

Introduction & Translation
BY ARNOLD J. TOYNBEE

Ipse Epicurus obit decurso lumine vitae,
Qui genus humanum ingenio superavit et omnis
Restinxit, stellas exortus ut aetherius sol.
Tu vero dubitabis et indignabere obire?

A MENTOR BOOK
Published by THE NEW AMERICAN LIBRARY;
New York and Toronto
The New English Library Limited, London

*Published as a MENTOR BOOK
by arrangement with Beacon Press,
who have authorized this softcover edition.*

SEVENTH PRINTING

Originally published by
J. M. Dent & Sons, Ltd., London, in the series
The Library of Greek Thought.

MENTOR TRADEMARK REG. U.S. PAT. OFF. AND FOREIGN COUNTRIES
REGISTERED TRADEMARK—MARCA REGISTRADA
HECHO EN CHICAGO, U.S.A.

MENTOR BOOKS are published *in the United States* by
The New American Library, Inc.,
1301 Avenue of the Americas, New York, New York 10019,
in Canada by The New American Library of Canada Limited,
295 King Street East, Toronto 2, Ontario,
in the United Kingdom by The New English Library Limited,
Barnard's Inn, Holborn, London, E.C. 1, England

FIRST PRINTING, DECEMBER, 1953

PRINTED IN THE UNITED STATES OF AMERICA

INTRODUCTION

THE present volume is complementary to the volume in the same series which deals with Ancient Greek, or Hellenic, *Historical Thought,* in the sense that the passages translated in either volume are largely drawn from the works of identical writers. If the reader asks why twice as much space should be devoted to historical literature as to certain other fields of Hellenic intellectual activity, the answer is twofold. In the first place, there is a practical reason, which may be stated very shortly. The literary remains of the Hellenic genius which Fortune has preserved to us in the historical field happen to be so much greater in bulk than the remains preserved in most other branches of literature, that it is hardly possible to do justice to them, by the method uniformly followed in this series, within anything like the same compass. There is also a second reason, of a theoretical kind, which may be worth consideration.

There are always two aspects from which historical literature must be regarded in order to be understood, and this is so because the historical thought of any given society—unlike (for example) the corresponding scientific thought—is, broadly speaking, introspective. It is directed, not toward the permanent physical environment of Mankind, but toward the life history of a particular civilization, and this implies a special relationship between the object of thought and the thought itself. On the one hand, the method, the results and, in general, the content of any historical thought naturally throw light upon the life of the society in which that thought has arisen; but also, conversely, a knowledge and appreciation of that society's character and career, as revealed through its historical thought, are essential for an understanding of the thought itself. Without this, it is difficult to seize the points of resemblance and difference between the historical thought of the society in question and the historical thought of other societies which have come and gone in other times and places under dissimilar conditions. Since the ultimate object of the present series is to enable English readers to take a comparative view of Hellenic and Modern Western thought in various fields, it is important to supply, as far as possible, whatever materials may be necessary to this end in each instance.

The bearing of historical experience upon historical thought is really almost too evident to need illustration. It lies to hand in the well-worn antithesis between the "Medieval Chronicle" and the characteristic works of Hellenic or, again, of Modern Western historical art. The Medieval Christian chronicler, Byzantine or Western,[1] was dominated in his historical thought by a social heritage which normally influenced his mind more

[1] And also their brother the Muslim chronicler, whose "Middle Ages" began about six centuries later than the "Middle Ages" of Byzantine and Western civilization, and are only just drawing to a close in our own times.

strongly than the direct experience of his own society. This heritage was embodied in an ancient religion which had embraced in its system almost every side of life, and which, among other things, impressed upon its latter-day followers a dogmatic view of History and a specifically theological interest in historical studies. For them, the History of Mankind appeared, through the Christian lens, as an interlude played, in Time, and upon the scene of This World, against an "other-worldly" background of Eternity. It began at a definite moment with the Creation[1] of the World; it was to end, equally abruptly, with the Last Judgment;[2] and it was divided into a "Time of Ignorance" and a "Time of Grace" as sharply as the Universe had been divided by the Creator, on the first day, into the two realms of light and darkness.[3]

Contrast this with the historical thought of Hellenism or of the Modern West, and the difference will be found to correspond with a difference in historical development. Apparently the Hellene had acquired little or no social heritage from his Minoan predecessors to help or hinder him, and his own experience was therefore not overshadowed and discounted by a tradition taken on trust at secondhand. If he were inspired to study and write the history of the society to which he belonged, his motive was not to illustrate an *a priori* scheme of salvation but to give expression, for the benefit of his contemporaries and successors, to an intellectual curiosity which had no external stimulus. His approach to historical writing lay through politics and not through theology; he had merely been diverted (by the chances and changes of this mortal life) from action to the study of action; he was not (like many Medieval historians) projecting an "other-worldly" scheme into a world of affairs in which he had never played a personal part; and he was led back into the study of the past chiefly by his eagerness to understand and explain the present, whereas the Medieval historian tended to think of the present in terms of the Last Judgment or of the Creation.

Similarly, we cannot analyze our own Modern Western historical outlook without some realization of the peculiar conditions under which it has been reached. It is the specific outlook of a society which has created Western music; invented infinitesimals and the mathematics of movement, change, and infinity; undergone the Industrial Revolution; and been converted to the doctrines of Nationality and Darwinism. Our present outlook was not anticipated by Hellenism, because the

[1] The Byzantine chroniclers reckoned by "the year so-and-so since the Creation of the World."

[2] The Nuremberg Chronicle leaves a few blank pages after the latest entry, and then anticipates the Last Judgment in a realistic woodcut on the final page of all.

[3] Most of these features reappeared in Islamic historical thought, owing to the fact that the dominant theology was derived from the same origins.

progress of Hellenic society happened to be arrested before it had achieved or suffered any of these particular experiences. On the other hand, there were elements in the Hellenic outlook which are foreign to us, because they were inspired by experiences which we have lacked or by sensibilities which we have not cultivated.

Thus the history and the historical thought of any society are more intimately related to one another than the scientific thought of a society is related to the permanent phenomena of the physical environment. It is possible, of course, that Hellenic or Western or Indian or Far Eastern scientific thought may throw light on the realities of physical nature, or, again, that these realities (assuming that there is any certain knowledge of them) may throw light back upon the processes of scientific thought. At the same time, the opposite possibilities have equally to be admitted. For example, most educated people in the Modern Western world believe that such systems of scientific thought as Magic, Astrology, Palmistry, and Enteroscopy,[1] so far from throwing light upon the facts of physical nature, bear no relation to them whatsoever, and positively militate against a correct understanding of them. Similarly, a knowledge of the facts of nature (if we may assume, for the sake of argument, that our Modern Western reading of these facts is substantially correct so far as it goes) may hinder rather than help the understanding of Hellenic or other non-Western systems of scientific theory, because it may mislead us into analyzing those systems according to their conformity or non-conformity with our own, when, all the time, their authors were looking out upon physical nature with different eyes than ours. In other words, a volume in this series dealing with Hellenic scientific thought would not necessarily gain anything from a companion volume setting forth objectively (if that were possible) the relevant facts regarding the permanent environment of the human race, whereas a supplement of this kind is almost indispensable to the reader when the object of the thought is not physical nature but human history. The present volume is an attempt to supply this need by presenting to English readers the object of Hellenic historical thought as seen through the eyes of Hellenic historians. Since the characteristics of these authors, and the methods followed by the present translator in attempting to render them in English, are discussed in the introduction to the volume dealing with *Historical Thought*, it would be superfluous

[1] The science of reading the future by killing an animal, cutting it open, and examining the shape and markings of its offal—all according to a certain rigidly prescribed religious ceremonial. This science obtained a great hold even over the educated classes of Hellenic society. It still flourishes in Mongolia, whither it presumably spread in the course of centuries, as it spread to Hellas, from its original home in Mesopotamia.

to touch upon these questions again, and there is nothing here to add except a brief explanation of the way in which the present volume is arranged.

Although this volume is related, in the sense which has just been explained, to the volume which deals with *Historical Thought*, it is intended to give an independent, though inevitably rather an impressionist, picture of Hellenic history. Every history is a growth, and every growth is a mysterious union of permanence and change—a foreground of change thrown up against a background of permanence, and then, in other phases, a foreground of permanence which masks unceasing changes behind the scenes. The two parts into which this volume is divided represent, in a general way, these two elements in its theme. The first part is occupied with the life history of Hellenic civilization,[1] its vicissitudes between genesis and extinction, or what, in the case of an individual human being, we should call his or her "career." This is the dramatic side of life, and also the side on which each particular life has most in common with every other. There is a fundamental similarity in all the plots, and probably a limit to the number of possible variations. These two features of movement and of universality are essential interests, without which the play would have little meaning for human spectators. On the other hand, these spectators would also find it savorless if the element of permanence were absent, for then the movement would be chaos and the universality a formula. There is no human interest in a "career" unless the subject of it is a "character," which maintains its self-identity through all its reactions to life and all the enlargement of its experience. Characters are something permanent, and they are something individual as well—as infinite as careers are limited in their variety.

The career or life history of Hellenism, to begin with this, was a movement in Time, and the first step toward surveying it is to determine its span. Can we date the span of Hellenism, from birth to death, with any precision? As a definite *terminus ante quem*, we might take the first and most critical siege of Constantinople by the Arabs, which probably occurred in the years 674-76 after Christ, and the failure of which insured that Byzantine civilization would not be stillborn. An equally definite *terminus post quem* would be the *Völkerwanderung* which was brought to a halt at the borders of Egypt about the year 1196 B.C., and which was probably the last scene in the breakup of Minoan society—the predecessor of Hellenism in

---

[1] Civilization and its sequel de-civilization are themselves essentially processes and not static conditions. In English, this fact is not necessarily implied in the structure of the words, but there is little implication in the original Latin, for Latin verbal nouns in *-atio* always connote action in their primary meanings.

the Aegean. Another scene in that great tragedy inspired the
heroic poetry of the Hellenic destroyers. Long after the con-
flagration kindled by them in other men's palaces had died
down into ashes, the memory of its dazzling brightness continued to guide their footsteps through an age of darkness
toward the gray glimmer of a new dawn; and in this sense
the Homeric Poems, like all genuine Epic, are the offspring of
a historical experience intensely taken to heart. Yet both these
dates belong (and that by very reason of their comparative
precision) to the history of worlds that came and went before
and after the world of Hellenism existed. All that can be said
is that the rise, the achievement, and the fall of Hellenism
occurred between them; and we must look to "internal evidence" for positive light upon the life history of this intervening civilization. The passages grouped under the title of "Civilization" in the present work are intended as a slight and
tentative guide in this field of exploration. We may be sure, at
any rate, that a kingdom is in its glory when the gentiles of the
hinterland press forward, at the hazard of their lives, in order
to take it by storm, and the first passage to be translated in this
group has therefore been the story of Scyles. Again, we may
be sure that the ship is sinking when the rats desert it for another, and the group therefore finds its natural close in Priscus's conversation with the nameless renegade at Attila's *ordu*.
When the door at last opens into Onegesius's *kibitka*, Priscus
glides through it, beyond the ken of Hellenism, into the Won-
derland of the Steppe, in which there is no change nor shadow
of turning from Scyles's day to Attila's or from Attila's to
Oubacha's.[1] Nomadism, a civilization as complex and as rigid
as the life of ants or bees, offers an admirable standard for
measuring the "duration" (in the Bergsonian sense) of Hellenism—a civilization from which it differed in almost every way,
but with which its destinies were linked by economic and
eventually by political relations. The Hellenized *khaqan* of the
Scythians and the Nomadized captive of the Huns represent
the respective generations in which Hellenism was unmistak-
ably on the upward and on the downward grade, and in the
span between them Hellas manifested all the potentialities for
good and evil in her genius. If Scyles's strait-laced tribesmen,
anticipating the Sleepers of Ephesus, could have taken their
seats, four centuries later, among their *louches* Parthian cous-
ins and have seen the head of Marcus Crassus flourished, in a
calculated Bacchic ecstasy, by a Hellenic play actor, they
would have shaken their own heads and have reflected how
right they had been in their estimate of the Dionysiac ritual. It
would have meant nothing to them that, while they had lain

[1] See De Quincey: *The Revolt of the Tartars* (Works, ed. by D. Masson, Vol.
VII.: London, 1897, Black).

sleeping all unconscious in their cave, the Dionysus of Athens had inspired Aeschylus and Sophocles and the author of the *Bacchae* himself with visions of truth and beauty of which neither the initiators of Scyles at Borysthenes nor the traducer of Euripides in Mesopotamia had ever dreamt. Indeed, could they have walked the earth again yet a century later, in order to converse with Paul of Tarsus at some street corner in the city which he had found "so terribly infested with images," they could have informed him of an equally shocking spectacle in the grounds of the mansion which their eccentric sovereign had built for himself in the farthest outpost of the Hellenic world. Paul, the Scythians, Surenas, and the author of the Second Book of Maccabees in conclave would have agreed that the works of Hellenism were in all places the same and at all times abominable.

We cannot, however, abandon Hellas to the judgment of her historical rivals without correcting our vision by the evidence of her sons. Democedes and Gillus, at any rate, in the sixth century B.C., felt that a life of exile from the *Piazza* was no life at all, whatever material inducements Oriental civilization might have to offer; and their homesickness finds a strange echo in the sixth century after Christ—an echo which intimates that Priscus's encounter with the renegade was not quite the last incident in the drama. Nearly eighty years after,[1] when Justinian enforced the laws against pagan worship and the Schools of Athens were closed by administrative action, the ejected professors—the last Seven Wise Men of Hellenic philosophy—resolved to journey eastward after the star of the philosopher-king, to see whether it would stand over the palace of Khosru Anushirwan at Ctesiphon. The tale is recorded by Agathias,[2] but it has not been translated here—partly because Agathias is no Herodotus and has left it to Gibbon[3] (who is accessible to all readers of English) to make the most of the story, and partly because this book has already reached its proper limits of size. Suffice it to say that the seven philosophers were disillusioned—as they could not fail to be, since they had elected to steer their course in the very teeth of the cyclone by which their sun was being obscured and their kingdom obliterated. The art which was replacing[4] the art of Phidias, the architecture which was replacing the architecture of the Parthenon, the religion which was replacing the religion of Pride and Doom and Envy—all, in that very generation, were pushing westward from their Syro-Iranian homes in a victorious invasion of the Hellenic world. Thus Khosru was an

---

[1] In A.D. 529.
[2] Book II, chapter 30.
[3] Chapter XL. in Vol. IV (pp. 261 seqq.) of Bury's smaller edition.
[4] See M. Rostovtzeff: *Iranians and Greeks in South Russia* (Oxford, 1922, Clarendon Press).

even more incongruous candidate for the role of Açoka than Plato himself had found in Dionysius II; but, although the Persian Padishah could not satisfy the philosophers' ideal, it must be recorded in justice to him that he did them a very good turn. In the peace negotiations of A.D. 533 between the Persian and the Roman governments, Khosru insisted on including a special clause guaranteeing to the voluntary but now sadly homesick exiles not merely re-admission to Roman territory but the right to cherish their special religious convictions for the remainder of their lives without being molested by Imperial authority. Thus, in the sixth century after Christ, as in the sixth century before Him, the children of Hellas found, *in partibus infidelium,* that they could not forget her. Changed though Athens would have been, almost beyond recognition, to Democedes's eyes, since the year which he had spent within her gates as medical officer to the Government of the Pisistratids, there was still something dear and indispensable about the city which could wring the hearts of the last Platonists and Aristotelians. No doubt a skeptic from the fifth century B.C. would have pronounced them to be laboring under the same delusion as Procopius, for, outside the lecture room, in their intimate thoughts and emotions, they were as hopelessly un-Hellenic as their Christian persecutors.

The second part, which deals with character, explains itself. The first section illustrates the psychology of the community or herd, and the second, the conscious conflict of individual wills. The conflict of wills is represented by examples of a literary artifice which is interesting to us, because it is a distinctive feature of Hellenic historical writing as contrasted with our own. The semi-fictitious speech (or thrust and parry of speeches drawn out into a debate) is clearly a dangerous instrument in a historian's hands, and yet we have discovered nothing equivalent to take its place. A Modern Western historian who wished to convey the state of opinion (say, in England) at some political crisis would probably take refuge in an appendix and would there reprint three speeches from *Hansard,* four leading articles from the London newspapers, and two from the provincial press; but this would not be a solution of the problem with which the Hellenic historians more boldly grappled. The materials for a work of art are not a substitute for the work itself. A series of snapshots, or even of studies, from different angles, does not supply the place of a portrait or a statue. The Hellenic method of portrayal may be excessively "idealized" or "subjective," but we have no right to criticize Solomon's architecture so long as we refuse, in our own case, to venture beyond the limits of David.

ARNOLD J. TOYNBEE.

LONDON.

PREFACE TO THE 1950 EDITION

MORE than a quarter of a century has now passed since I translated the passages assembled in this volume and wrote the introduction, and during these intervening twenty-six years the waters of our own Western history have rolled on with a gathering impetus. A second world war has followed the first, and in A.D. 1950 we can perhaps see whither we are heading rather more clearly than we could in A.D. 1924. At any rate, there is a more vivid and more widespread realization in our Western world today than there was then of the historical truth that we are living through a time of decision, and that the choices which we are having to make in our generation are momentous. We are aware that it is all-important for us to choose right, and that our chances of success depend largely on our ability to make right estimates of the alternative courses before us. What light have we that we can project upon the darkness of the future? We have the precious light of experience, which has always been Mankind's guide to action in public, as in private, affairs. No sensible person, of course, has ever imagined that a mechanical application of past experience to present problems will grind out automatic solutions of these. Experience gives us enigmatic hints, not blueprinted instructions. Yet these hints are invaluable, since they are the only light on the future that we can bring to bear; and, where the future that is in question is a society's, not an individual's, the experience of other societies has the same significance for us as the experience of our contemporaries and our elders in the ordering of our personal lives.

The experience of the Hellenic society—the Graeco-Roman world—is particularly illuminating from this point of view, because the Greeks' and Romans' experience is now over—their world is now dead—and, in consequence, we know the plot of that play from beginning to end, in sharp contrast to our ignorance of what lies before ourselves in a play which is still being acted, and in which we living actors have all the time to improvise our parts.

For this reason, Greek and Roman history is perpetually gaining in interest for us as it is receding in time. Every passing year of our own history that makes Greek and Roman history chronologically more remote brings it closer to us psychologically. If there is any key to the riddle of our destiny, that key lies here, I believe; and, believing this, I find the fascination of Greek and Roman history always growing greater for me as I live through one decade after another of the formidable contemporary history of the Modern world.

1950.   A. J. T.

CONTENTS

CONTENTS

PART II—CHARACTER

SECTION I—SOCIAL PSYCHOLOGY

SECTION II—CONFLICTS OF WILL

PART I

CIVILIZATION

GREEK CIVILIZATION AND CHARACTER

THE PROSELYTE
(*ca.* 450-440 B.C.)
(HERODOTUS OF HALICARNASSUS: Book IV, chapters 78-80)

ARIOPÍTHES, king of the nomads, had several sons, one of whom was Scyles. Scyles's mother was a Hellene from Istria [1] without a drop of native blood in her veins, and she instructed him personally in the Greek language and gave him a Hellenic education. Some time after this, Ariopíthes fell by treachery at the hands of Spargapíthes, king of the Agathyrsi,[2] and Scyles inherited his father's kingdom, as well as his wife, whose name was Opoea.[3] Though he thus found himself king of the nomads, Scyles could not reconcile himself to the nomadic life, but was far more strongly attracted by Hellenic civilization in consequence of the education that he had received—an inclination which he sought to satisfy in the following way. Whenever he conducted his nomad horde to the town of Borysthenes,[4] he used to leave the horde in the suburbs and enter the town by himself. As soon as he was safe inside the walls and had closed the gates behind him, he would put on Hellenic clothes and pass the time of day in the *piazza* in this dress without a bodyguard or any paraphernalia.[5] In fact, he would live exactly like a Hellene and perform his religious duties according to the Hellenic ritual. Then, after spending a month or more in the place, he would put on his nomad clothes again and go away. He frequently repeated this

[1] A Hellenic commercial settlement on the Dobruja coast of the Black Sea, in the neighborhood of the modern Costanza. [ED.]
[2] Another nomadic people occupying the Steppe of Hungary, to the west of Ariopíthes's nomads, whose pastures lay in southern Russia. [ED.]
[3] Opoea was a native, and she had borne to Ariopíthes a son called Oricus. [AUTHOR.]
[4] The Hellenes of Borysthenes claim to be of Milesian origin. [AUTHOR.]
A Hellenic commercial settlement, *alias* Olbia, at the mouth of the River Bug. [ED.]
[5] They picketed the gates to make sure that no nomad should see him wearing this costume. [AUTHOR.]

17

experiment until eventually he built himself a house in Borysthenes and married a Borysthenite wife to keep it for him.
Evil had, however, to befall Scyles, and it availed itself of the
following opportunity. Scyles had conceived a desire to be
initiated into the sacraments of Bacchic Dionysus, and he was
on the point of applying himself to the necessary ritual when
he was visited by an impressive portent. He possessed in
Borysthenes a large and sumptuous mansion[1] which stood in
its own grounds and was surrounded by sphinxes and griffins
of white marble. This mansion was struck by a thunderbolt
and burnt to the ground, but the event did not in the least
deter Scyles from completing his ritual. When Scyles had
duly received the Bacchic initiation, however, a citizen of
Borysthenes made use of the fact to give a shock to the
nomads.[2] "Of course," he said, "you nomads laugh at us because we go into Bacchic ecstasy and allow the God to possess
us; but now this divinity has taken possession of your king as
well. He is going into ecstasy and being driven insane by the
God. If you do not believe me, come with me and I will show
you." The leading nomads did go with him, and the citizen
conducted them secretly to the top of a tower and posted
them there. When Scyles passed by in the congregation of
the initiated and the nomads saw him going into ecstasy, they
took it as a calamity of the gravest kind and hastened out of
the town to announce what they had seen to the whole horde.
When Scyles started out, after this incident, for his own
camping grounds, the nomads took his brother Octamasades[3]
as their leader and rose in rebellion. Discovering the action
that was being taken against him and the reason for it, Scyles
sought an asylum in Thrace, upon the receipt of which information Octamasades marched against Thrace with his own
forces. On the line of the Danube the Thracians opposed his
advance, and an engagement was imminent when Sitalces[4] sent
a note to Octamasades to the following effect: "It is absurd
that we should engage in hostilities with one another. You are
my sister's son and you hold a brother of mine in your hands.
Surrender him to me and I promise to extradite your Scyles;
but do not let either of us risk the arbitrament of war." Sitalces
sent this note to Octamasades with a proposal for an armistice;
and Octamasades agreed to his conditions,[5] gave up his own
maternal uncle to Sitalces and so got possession of Scyles.

[1] The house to which I have referred a few lines above. [AUTHOR.]
[2] It should be noted that the nomads regard the Bacchic cult as a blot upon
Hellenic civilization, and argue that it is improper to invent a God who induces
insanity in human beings. [AUTHOR.]
[3] Octamasades's mother was the daughter of Tereus (king of the Odrysae in
Thrace). [AUTHOR.]
[4] King of the Odrysae and maternal uncle of Octamasades. [ED.]
[5] It was perfectly true that a brother of Sitalces had taken asylum from that
monarch at Octamasades's court. [AUTHOR.]

Sitalces took over his brother and carried him off, while Octamasades beheaded Scyles on the spot. That is how the nomads safeguard their own institutions and how they punish tribesmen who attempt to improve upon them by adopting foreign observances.

THE PIAZZA FROM INSIDE
(*ca.* 519-515 B.C.)

(HERODOTUS: Book III, chapters 129-138)

NOT long after the safe arrival of Oroetes's[1] property at Susa, Darius happened to sprain his foot while out hunting, by dismounting too vigorously from the saddle. The sprain proved to be somewhat severe—in fact, there was a dislocation. Having always supposed that he had retained at his court the most distinguished members of the Egyptian medical profession, the King placed himself in their hands; but the Egyptians racked and wrenched the foot with no effect except to make things worse. The accident cost Darius seven sleepless days and nights, until on the eighth day (by which time he was in a bad way) somebody who had read rumors at Sardis, long before, regarding the skill of Democedes of Croton, reported these to his master. Darius ordered Democedes to be brought before him immediately. He was discovered lying neglected in some corner among Oroetes's slaves, and was brought into the King's presence trailing chains and clad in rags. When he had been placed in position, the King asked him whether he were skilled in his profession. Democedes refused to admit the fact, in terror lest he might be cut off from Hellas forever if he gave himself away. Darius, however, divined his professional skill and ordered his guards to bring whips and spikes on to the scene. At this point, Democedes gave himself away so far as to declare that, although he possessed no scientific knowledge, he had received a superficial professional training through having worked with a physician. The King then gave him a free hand, and Democedes applied Hellenic methods and substituted soothing for violent treatment, with the result that he enabled him to sleep again and that before long he had effected a cure—and this when the King had resigned himself to the prospect of being lame for life. After that, the King presented him with two pairs of golden fetters, which drew

[1] The Persian Pasha of Sardis who had trapped Polycrates during the reign of Cambyses and who had subsequently been destroyed by Darius for having attempted to establish his independence during the troubles at the beginning of Darius's reign. [ED.]

from Democedes the inquiry whether His Majesty were deliberately doubling his misfortunes in return for the cure. Darius was delighted at the *mot* and sent him off to call upon his womenfolk. When the eunuchs ushered him in, they announced to the women that this was the gentleman who had restored the King to life, whereupon each of them ladled into her money chest with a bowl and presented Democedes with such a lavish testimonial that the coins which fell from the bowls and which were picked up by Sciton, the doctor's servant, as he followed at his heels, produced him a prodigious fortune.

The circumstances which had brought Democedes from his home in Croton to the court of Polycrates were as follows. At Croton he was saddled with an ill-tempered father, and when he could bear him no longer, he left him to himself and went off to Aegina. There he established himself and, by the end of his first year's practice, he had left all the local doctors behind, though he had no equipment nor any medical instruments. In his second year the Aeginetan Government employed him on the public account at a salary of one talent; in his third year the Athenian Government employed him at one hundred minas; and in his fourth year Polycrates at two talents. This was how Democedes came to Samos, and it is principally owing to him that the Crotoniate school of medicine has achieved its reputation.[1] Finally, after curing Darius, Democedes found himself the possessor of a large mansion at Susa and an honored guest at the King's table—in fact, he had no wish unsatisfied except the single desire to go home to Hellas. One thing that he did was to intercede successfully with the King on behalf of the Egyptian physicians who had been treating the King before and who were under sentence of impalement for having been put to shame by a Hellenic confrere. Another was to rescue an Elean diviner who had been in the suite of Polycrates and who had since lain neglected among the slaves.[2] Indeed, Democedes was something tremendous in the King's estimation.

Not long after this, another incident occurred. Queen Atossa[3] was troubled by a growth on her breast which eventually ulcerated and began to spread. So long as it was a comparatively trifling matter, modesty prevented her from taking anybody into her confidence, but when she was in a bad way, she called in Democedes and showed the place to him. Demo-

---

[1] This was at the time when the medical school of Croton was regarded as the best and that of Cyrene as the second-best in Hellas, while during the same period Argos was reputed to be the leading country for music. [COMMENTATOR.]

[2] The non-Samian members of Polycrates's suite (including Democedes himself) had been reduced to slavery by Oroetes and subsequently brought to Susa with the rest of Oroetes's property, after its confiscation by Darius. [ED.]

[3] Cyrus's daughter and Darius's wife. [AUTHOR.]

cedes guaranteed to cure her, but made her swear to do him, in return, whatever service he might ask of her—adding that he should ask nothing improper. He then proceeded to treat her and duly effected a cure—the consequence of which was that, acting under Democedes's instructions, Atossa approached Darius, one night in bed, with the following suggestion:

"Sire, with this immense power of yours, why do you sit idle, without increasing either the territory or the power of the Persian Empire? Surely a man in the prime of life, who is master of vast resources, ought to make his mark in active achievement if the Persians are to realize the fact that they have a man for their ruler. Incidentally, a forward policy would kill two birds with one stone; for, besides teaching the Persians that they have a man in authority over them, it would grind them down with military service and leave them no leisure to plot against your government. At present you have the chance of achieving something, while you are in your prime. As the body matures, the mind keeps pace with it; but it also keeps pace with its decay, and then its edge is blunted for every form of activity."

When the Queen had offered these remarks· according to instructions, the King made the following rejoinder:

"My dear, you have precisely anticipated what is in my own mind. I have decided to throw a bridge across from this continent to the other and to make an expedition against the nomads. It will not be long before this is completed."

"Listen to me," said Atossa. "It is better to give up the idea of marching first against the nomads. The nomads are fruit that will fall into your lap whenever you choose. Please me by turning your arms first against Hellas. I have heard accounts of the women and have set my heart on having Laconian and Argive and Attic and Corinthian maids. You have at court the most ideal man in the world for showing you round Hellas and acting as your guide—the man who cured your foot."

"My dear," replied Darius, "since it is evidently your pleasure that I should attack Hellas first, I think the best initial step will be to send some Persians into Hellas as spies and to attach to them the man you mention. They shall use their eyes and their intelligence and shall report to us upon the situation there in detail. Then I shall be able to turn my energies against Hellas with full knowledge of the facts."

These were Darius's words, and it was no sooner said than done. At streak of dawn, he summoned fifteen distinguished Persians and instructed them to go with Democedes and survey the littoral of Hellas. They were to be sure not to allow Democedes to give them the slip. At all costs, they were to bring him back again. After he had given his instructions to these gentlemen, his next step was to summon Democedes himself and to request him to act as guide to the Persians, to show them round the whole of Hellas, and then to return to Susa. As presents for his father and brothers he told him to take with him all the furniture in his house, which he promised to replace many times over. In addition, as a contribution to the presents, he promised him a merchantman, with a fine cargo of assorted goods, which was to sail in his convoy. Darius, in my belief, had no insidious purpose in making him these offers, but Democedes was afraid that the King might be setting a trap for him. Accordingly, he did not show *empressement* in accepting all these proffered gifts, but proposed to leave his personal possessions where they were, in order that he might find them when he came back again. He signified, however, his acceptance of the merchantman which Darius offered him toward the present for his brothers. After giving the same instructions to Democedes as to the Persians, Darius despatched the party to the coast. They struck it in Phoenicia or, to be precise, at the Phoenician city of Sidon, where they at once manned two warships and freighted a great galleon as well with a fine assortment of goods.

When they had completed their arrangements, they set sail for Hellas, came inshore, inspected the littoral and kept a record of their survey, until, after inspecting the greater number (including the most notable) of the Hellenic countries, they arrived at Tarentum in Italy. At Tarentum, out of complaisance toward Democedes, the king of the country, Aristophilides, first dislocated the steering gear of the Persian ships and then interned the Persians themselves on the ground that they were spies. While his companions were undergoing this experience, Democedes arrived at Croton and, as soon as he had reached his home, Aristophilides released the Persians and returned to them the fittings which he had confiscated. So the Persians sailed on from Tarentum in pursuit of Democedes until they arrived at Croton, where they found him passing the time of day in the *piazza* and attempted to arrest him. Some of the citizens were in such terror of the Persian power that they were prepared to sacrifice him, but others stood by him and began to belabor the Persians with their sticks, in spite of their representations. "Gentlemen," the Persians protested, "take care what you are doing. You are shielding from the law a runaway slave of the King's. How can King Darius be expected to stomach such an affront as this? Or how can you justify your action if you drive us away? Do you suppose that this will not be the first country against which we shall march and the first which we shall attempt to carry captive?" Their arguments, however, did not have the desired effect upon the Crotoniates. The Persians were not only prevented from recovering Democedes but were deprived of the galleon which they were convoying; whereupon they started on their homeward voyage to Asia, without any longer attempting to explore the remoter parts of Hellas now that they had lost their guide. When they put to sea, Democedes did give them one injunction. They were to tell Darius that he (Democedes) had become engaged to be married to Milo's daughter.[1]

After putting to sea from Croton, the Persians suffered shipwreck on the coast of Iapygia,[2] where they were reduced to slavery and subsequently ransomed by an exiled citizen of Tarentum named Gillus, who brought them home to Darius. In return for this service, the King was prepared to offer to Gillus whatever Gillus himself might desire. Gillus chose to be repatriated to Tarentum, after first explaining his misfortune. He was anxious, however, not to bring trouble upon Hellas by causing a great armada to sail, on his account, for Italy, and therefore declared himself satisfied if the task of restoring him to his home might be entrusted exclusively to the people of Cnidus. Knowing that there was an *entente* between the governments of Tarentum and Cnidus, he thought that the latter would have the best chance of repatriating him. Darius's promise was followed by performance. He sent instructions to the government of Cnidus to restore Gillus to Tarentum, which the Cnidians did their best to carry out. They failed, however, to carry the Tarentine government with them and were not in a position to use force. This concludes the story, which explains who were the first Persians to visit Hellas from Asia and what was the reason for their coming in the role of spies.

THE PIAZZA FROM OUTSIDE
(*ca.* 545 B.C.)
(HERODOTUS: BOOK I, chapters 152-153)

THE Ionian and Aeolian mission arrived at Sparta,[3] and selected Pythermus, the Phocaean representative, as their principal spokesman. This gentleman put on a scarlet coat (in the hope of drawing the maximum number of Spartiates to his meeting at the news of this sensation), took his stand, and

---

[1] The athlete Milo enjoyed immense prestige with the King, and I believe that Democedes's motive in throwing himself into this marriage (which cost him a fortune) was a desire to make himself appear, in Darius's eyes, as a person of importance in his own country as well as abroad. [AUTHOR.]

[2] The Heel of Italy. [ED.]

[3] The rate at which events were moving was extremely rapid. [AUTHOR.]

started to deliver a long speech demanding Spartan intervention in his countrymen's favor. The Lacedaemonians not only paid no attention to him but rejected the suggestion that they should intervene, so the mission left the country. Although, however, they had rebuffed the Ionian mission, the Lacedaemonians did go so far as to send a "fifty-oar" with representatives of Sparta on board who were intended, in my belief, to spy into the position of Cyrus and the state of Ionia. When this Lacedaemonian mission arrived at Phocaea, they sent Lācrinēs, their most distinguished member, on to Sardis, in order to deliver to Cyrus[1] a *note verbale* from the Lacedaemonians, warning him not to molest any community belonging to the Hellenic world or Sparta would interfere. When the envoy had recited this message, Cyrus is reported to have asked the Hellenic members of his suite who on earth the Lacedaemonians were and what was their man power, that they should lay down the law to him in this way. While making this inquiry, he remarked to the Spartiate envoy: "I have never yet felt afraid of people who have a place reserved in the center of their towns for meeting together and cheating one another on oath. Unless there is something wrong with me, these people shall soon have troubles of their own to make their tongues wag, without needing the troubles of the Ionians." These words of Cyrus were a hit at the Hellenes in general, in allusion to their custom of laying out *piazze* where they buy and sell. The Persians, in contrast, have no use for *piazze* and the institution itself is quite unfamiliar to them.

"THE FOOLS WERE RIGHT"[2]
(480 B.C.)
(HERODOTUS: Book VII, chapters 101-105)

WHEN Xerxes had completed his inspection of the military and naval forces[3] and had disembarked, he sent for Damaratus[4] son of Ariston, who was serving on his staff for the campaign against Hellas, and called him up to ask him a question. "Damaratus," he said, "there is a particular question which it is

[1] Cyrus the Great of Persia, who had just (*ca.* 545 B.C.) conquered Lydia, the former suzerain of the Hellenic communities along the western littoral of the Anatolian mainland, of which Lydia was the hinterland. [ED.]

[2] "All the wise men were on one side and all the damned fools were on the other, and by Gad, Sir, the damned fools were right."—Duke of Wellington. [ED.]

[3] The scene of this episode was the plain of Doriscus on the littoral of Western Thrace (approximately at Dedeagach), when Xerxes was marching against Hellas with his Grand Army in the spring of 480 B.C. [ED.]

[4] An ex-King of Sparta who had been deprived of his throne by the intrigues of his personal and political enemies at home and had found an asylum in the Persian dominions. [ED.]

my pleasure at this moment to put to you. You are a Hellene, and also (as I understand from you yourself as well as from the other Hellenes who have audience with me) you are a citizen of no mean or puny city. I therefore desire you now to inform me whether the Hellenes will have the courage to offer me resistance. I believe I am right in thinking that even if all the Hellenes in the world and all the populations of the countries lying to the west of them were to unite their forces, they would not possess the military strength to oppose my invasion —short of a *union sacrée*. At the same time, I should be glad to hear your opinion on the point, as it strikes you yourself." Damaratus's rejoinder to this question was: "Sire, am I to tell you what is true or what will please you?" Xerxes commanded him to tell the truth and promised that he would like him not a whit the less for doing so. Upon receiving this assurance, Damaratus continued as follows: "Sire, you have commanded me to tell the truth at all costs and to the bitter end and to give you information which will not entitle you, in the light of future events, to call me a liar. Well, I will do so! Hellas, Sire, has poverty always with her. Poverty has been her foster sister from infancy, while Honor is an import, artificially created by deep thinking and strenuous legislation. These are the weapons with which Hellas keeps Poverty and Despotism from her door. I have an admiration for all the Hellenic populations of the so-called Dorian countries, but for the present purpose I am going to confine my remarks to the Lacedaemonians, and this for two reasons—the first being that they cannot conceivably accept your proposals (involving, as they do, the enslavement of Hellas), and the second that they will assuredly measure swords with you, even if every other Hellenic people takes your side. In regard to the question of numbers, it would be irrelevant to inquire whether they possess the man power demanded by such a policy. If they turn out (say) a thousand strong, the thousand will fight you, and if the figure is smaller or greater than that, they will fight you just the same." This made Xerxes laugh. "My dear Damaratus," he observed, "what a preposterous assertion! A thousand men fight an army as strong as ours! Come now, tell me, you who profess to have been king of these people yourself: Will you, then, undertake here and now to fight against ten men? After all, if your rank and file come up, to a man, to the standard that you describe, you, who are their king, ought to be a match for twice as many antagonists as your subjects, according to the principles of your own Spartan constitution. If each individual Spartan is a match for ten soldiers of my army, then I shall expect you to be a match for twenty. At the same time, if your countrymen who make these extravagant pretensions possess anything like the same character and physique as you yourself and the other Hellenes who have audience with me, you may find—I warn you—that your present assertion is an empty boast. Let me place the question in a strictly rational light. How could resistance be offered to an army as strong as ours by a thousand or ten thousand or fifty thousand troops who were one and all of them free agents instead of being under the orders of a single commander? Assuming that there are five thousand of them, that means that we are putting more than a thousand men into the field to every one of theirs. Besides, troops subject (as troops are under our system) to the orders of a single commander would be inspired by dread of the latter with an artificial courage and would be driven by the compulsion of the lash to attack superior numbers, while if control were abandoned and they were left to their own sweet will, they would be incapable of both these efforts. Indeed, it is my personal opinion that even if the numerical disparity were removed and the Hellenes had the Persians alone to deal with, they would find it no joke to cross swords with them. As a matter of fact, the prowess of which you boast is a reality among us, though, so far from being common, it is rare. There are, however, Persians in my guard who will undertake to fight three Hellenic soldiers simultaneously single-handed. Evidently you are unaware of their existence or you would not talk such arrant nonsense."—"Sire," Damaratus retorted, "I knew all along that if I told you the truth I should not be telling you what you wished to hear. It is you, Sire, who, by forcing me to tell the absolute truth, have elicited from me the facts appertaining to the Spartans. You yourself know as well as anybody what an affection I happen to cherish, at this particular moment, for these countrymen of mine who have stripped me of my rank and ancestral prerogatives and have turned me into a homeless refugee—a refugee to whom your father, in his generous hospitality, gave subsistence and shelter. A right-thinking man could never possibly rebuff kindness shown to him, for which he is bound, on the contrary, to be profoundly grateful. I do not guarantee my own ability to fight ten men or two. I should not go out of my way to engage even in a single combat. If, however, I were put to it or if something important hung upon the issue which spurred me on, I should fight with the best will in the world against one of these soldiers who profess themselves singly a match for three Hellenes. This applies equally to the Lacedaemonians, who in fighting man to man are certainly second to none, while as a body they are the best fighters in the world. Free though they are, they are not free altogether. They too serve a master in the shape of Law, whom they dread far more intensely than your servants dread you. They show this by doing whatever their master orders, and his orders are always the same: 'In action it is forbidden to retire in the face of enemy forces of whatever strength. Troops are to keep their formation and to conquer or die.' If my assertions appear to you to be nonsense, I should prefer to keep my own counsel for the future, and I have only spoken now under compulsion. I only pray, Sire, that your hopes may be fulfilled."

This retort of Damaratus was treated by Xerxes as a joke. He was not in the least put out, and dismissed his interlocutor graciously.

SPARTA
(480 B.C.)
(HERODOTUS: Book VII, chapters 201-232)

KING XERXES was now encamped in the Trāchinian district of Mālis and the Hellenes in the pass,[1] which meant that Xerxes was in occupation of everything to the north of of Trāchis and the Hellenes of everything to the south and southwest in this corner of the continent. The Hellenic forces that were waiting to receive the Persian in this position were the following: 300 Spartan infantry; 1000 Tegēans and Mantinēans in equal contingents; 120 troops from Arcadian Orchomenos, and 1000 from the rest of Arcadia (which concludes the Arcadian contingent); 400 from Corinth, 200 from Phlīus; 80 Mycenaeans (which concludes the Peloponnesian contingent); and from Boeotia 700 Thespians and 400 Thebans. These contingents had been reinforced by a levy en masse of the Opuntian Locrians and by 1000 Phocians, both called up for the occasion. This had been done on their own initiative by the Hellenic forces, who had sent messages to the effect that they themselves had arrived as an advance guard of the main army; that the rest of the Confederate army was to be expected any day; and that the defense of the sea, which was being held by the Athenians, Aeginētans, and other naval members of the Confederacy, had been provided for, so that the local population had nothing to fear. The invader of Hellas was not a God but a man, and there never was nor had been mortal creature exempt from the taint of original misfortune—the greater misfortune the greater the personage. The present aggressor, being a mortal, was therefore bound to see his expectations falsi-

[1] The locality is called Thermopylae by the majority of Hellenes, and Pylae by the local inhabitants and their neighbors. [AUTHOR.] Pylae = Gates; Thermopylae = Warm Gates, in allusion to a hot sulphur spring at the western end of the pass. For the topography, see *Graecia*, edited by G. B. Grundy, in "Murray's Handy Classical Maps," and G. B. Grundy's book, *The Great Persian War*. [ED.]

fied. On the strength of these representations, the local nationalities had joined forces with the Confederates at Trachis. The contingent of each state was under its own commander, but the officer who enjoyed the greatest prestige and who was in general command of the force was the Lacedaemonian Leonidas.[1] On the present occasion, this officer had marched to Thermopylae with a picked body of 300 men who had reached their prime and who were leaving children behind them. On his way, he had called up the Thebans whom I have mentioned in my return and who were under the command of Leontiadas, son of Eurymachus. The motive of Leonidas in insisting upon taking these Thebans[2] with him was his strong suspicion that they were pro-Persian. He had therefore called them up for active service in order to see whether they would furnish him with a contingent or would openly refuse to join the Hellenic Confederacy, and the Thebans had furnished a contingent, though disingenuously. The troops with Leonidas had been sent in advance by the Spartan Government in order that the sight of them might induce the other Allies to march and deter them from going over to the enemy, as they might do (like their [northern] neighbors) if they heard that the Spartans were procrastinating. Eventually, when the obstacle of the Carnēan festival had been surmounted, the Spartans intended to terminate the celebrations, leave a garrison in their home country, and go to the front in full strength by forced marches. The rest of the Allies had likewise decided upon an identical procedure. A celebration of the Olympian Games happened to coincide with the events under consideration. They never expected that the operations at Thermopylae would reach their decision so rapidly as they actually did, and this was how they had come to be sending the advance guard.

While the Confederate governments had decided upon the course of action just indicated, the Hellenic forces at Thermopylae, now that the Persians had arrived in the immediate neighborhood of the passage, lost their nerve and held a council of war to discuss the possibility of withdrawal. The majority of the Peloponnesians were in favor of withdrawing to the Peloponnese and holding the line of the Isthmus of Corinth, but when Leonidas saw the indignation aroused among the Phocians and Locrians by this proposition, he moved that they should hold their ground and should send despatches to the Confederate states demanding reinforcements, in view of the inadequacy of their numbers for repulsing the Mede.[3] While

---

[1] The author's note on the genealogy and personal antecedents of King Leonidas has been omitted. [ED.]

[2] The only Hellenes upon whom he exercised any such pressure. [AUTHOR.]

[3] "Mede" is used as a synonym for "Persian," the Medes being a kindred nationality whose empire the Persians had inherited and enlarged. [ED.]

they were holding this council, Xerxes sent a cavalry scout to see how many they were and what they were doing. Before leaving Thessaly, he had heard that a small force had assembled at this point and that it was under the leadership of the Lacedaemonians and Leonidas, a descendant of Heracles. When the trooper rode up to the camp, he was unable to overlook and observe the whole of it, since the troops posted inside the wall, which they had thrown up and were now holding, were not within his field of vision. He was able, however, to reconnoiter the troops outside, who were posted in advance of the wall—a position which happened at the moment to be occupied by the Lacedaemonians. There he saw some of the men taking exercise and others combing their hair. Filled with amazement by what he observed, he proceeded to note their strength, and, when he had made an accurate note of everything, he rode back at his own pace—for nobody offered to pursue him and his appearance was received with profound indifference. He went off to make a full report to Xerxes of what he had seen, and when Xerxes heard it, he could not comprehend the situation. The enemy were evidently preparing to do—with all their might—and die; and, since their conduct struck him as ridiculous, he sent for Damaratus, son of Ariston, who was with the army. When Damaratus presented himself, Xerxes began to interrogate him on the details of the report with a view to discovering what the Lacedaemonians were about. "Once before," observed Damaratus, "when we were on the march against Hellas, you heard me on the subject of my countrymen, and on that occasion you made fun of me for telling you the outcome which I foresaw for your enterprise. In dealing with you, Sire, I find the practice of veracity an almost superhuman effort. Still, listen once again: These men have come to fight us for the possession of the pass and are making their preparations for doing so. They have a law to the following effect: At a moment when they are going to risk their lives, they brush their hair. Let me tell you that if you conquer these troops and the reserve at Sparta, then, Sire, there is no other nation in the world that will venture to offer you resistance. You are now encountering the finest kingdom and the best soldiers in Hellas." Xerxes was filled with incredulity by Damaratus's statements, and proceeded to ask him in the second place what tactics so tiny a force would be able to employ against his own army. "Sire," said Damaratus, "you may treat me as a liar if the outcome is not as I say."

Damaratus's words left Xerxes unconvinced, and he therefore allowed four days to pass in the constant expectation that his opponents would run away. On the fifth day, however, when, so far from decamping, the Hellenes persisted in com-

mitting what Xerxes regarded as the ostentatious folly of holding their ground, the King lost his temper and sent the Medes
and Cissians[1] to deal with them, with orders to arrest them and
bring them into his presence. When the Medes came into collision with the Hellenes, they suffered heavy casualties, but the
gaps were filled by reinforcements and they refused to retire
in spite of their disastrous failure. They made it obvious, however, to anyone with eyes to see, and not least to the King
himself, that there were many troops but few men. The action
continued throughout the day, and when the Medes were being
roughly handled, they eventually fell back and the attack was
carried on by the Persians for whom the King's name was
"Immortals" and who were under Hydarnes's command. These
picked troops were expected to settle the business with ease;
but, as soon as they made contact with the Hellenes in their
turn, they scored no better a success than the Median force but
had precisely the same experience. The fact was that they were
fighting in a defile, that they were equipped with shorter spears
than the Hellenes, and that they were unable to take advantage
of their numbers. The Lacedaemonians fought magnificently.
In every respect they acquitted themselves as professional soldiers among amateurs, but their most effective ruse was to turn
tail and pretend to flee in a body. At the spectacle of this, the
Orientals would come on with a shout and a clatter, whereupon the Lacedaemonians, when on the point of being overtaken, would turn about, present a front to the enemy, and lay
low in this maneuver an innumerable quantity of Persians. A
few casualties were also suffered in this action by the Spartans
themselves. The Persians failed to gain any ground in the pass,
though they attempted it in alternate companies and employed
every variety of tactics in their attack, until finally they retreated to the rear.[2] These were the results of the first day's
fighting; and on the day following the Orientals resumed the
struggle with no better fortune. They had counted, in going
into action, upon the paucity of their opponents' numbers and
expected to find them disabled by wounds and therefore incapable of offering further resistance. The Hellenes, however,
were organized in separate battalions, by nationalities, which
fought in rotation—with the exception of the Phocians, who
had been specially posted on the mountain to guard the footpath. Finding no change from their experiences of the previous
day, the Persians beat a retreat.

The King was in perplexity as to how he was to deal with

[1] The troops of Elam or Anshan, one of the home provinces of the Achaemenid
Dynasty which contained their capital, Susa (= the modern province of Ahwaz).
[ED.]
[2] In the course of these successive assaults, of which the battle consisted, it is
reported that the King, who was watching, three times leapt up from his throne
in terror for the safety of his army. [AUTHOR.]

the situation in which he found himself, when a Malian named Epialtas, son of Eurydāmus, obtained an interview with him, in the expectation of receiving a great reward, and informed him of the existence of the path leading to Thermopylae over the mountain—a piece of intelligence by which he caused the death of the Hellenes who had held their ground in this position.[1] Xerxes was so delighted with the results promised by Epialtas that, in his enthusiasm, he despatched Hydarnes and the troops under his command forthwith, and they left camp about dusk.[2] After crossing the Asōpus, they marched all night along the path (the topography of which is described in the footnote) with the Oetaean mountains on their right and the Trachinian on their left. Dawn was just glimmering when they reached the summit of the pass. This position was held, as I have explained above, by 1000 Phocian infantry, who, in guarding the path, were defending their own country.[3] The Persians had scaled the mountain without being detected under cover of the oak woods with which the whole landscape was clothed, and the Phocians only discovered the movement when it had been completed. It was a windless night and they heard a loud rustling, as was inevitable when the troops were marching over a bed of fallen leaves. The Phocians sprang up and had just begun to put on their equipment when the Orientals

[1] At a later date, fear of the Lacedaemonians induced Epialtas to take refuge in Thessaly, and, after he had done so, a price was set upon his head by the Assembly of the Amphictyonic League in one of its annual sessions at Thermopylae. Eventually, when he had been rash enough to return to Anticyra, he met his death at the hands of a Trachinian named Athānadas. Although Athānadas killed Epialtas for an irrelevant reason, which I shall explain in a later chapter, he was decorated by the Spartans all the same. That was how Epialtas subsequently met his end; but there is another story current to the effect that a Carystian named Onētes, son of Phānagoras, and an Anticyran named Corydallus, were the individuals who gave this information to the King and who guided the Persians round the mountain. I find this latter story quite unconvincing for two reasons: first, the deduction to be drawn from the fact that the representatives of Hellas in the Assembly set their price upon the head of Epialtas of Trachis and not upon the heads of Onetes and Corydallus, and the Assembly may surely be presumed to have made the most accurate inquiries possible; in the second place, the circumstance that we know Epialtas to have been specifically charged with the offense. The non-Malian nationality of Onetes certainly proves nothing, for he might still have been acquainted with this footpath if he had familiarized himself with the country. However, there is really no doubt that Epialtas was the individual who showed the way round the mountain by the footpath, and I have no hesitation in affixing the guilt to him. [AUTHOR.]

[2] This footpath had been discovered by the local Malians, and the first use that they had made of their discovery had been to show the Thessalians the way to attack the Phocians at a time when the Phocians had blocked the passage [of Thermopylae] with a wall and had thereby screened themselves against invasion. The sinister possibilities of the footpath had thus been discovered by the Malians long before Xerxes's campaign. To turn to the topography, the path begins at the River Asopus (which flows through the gorge) and, like the mountain over which it runs, is called Anopaea. This path of Anopaea stretches along a crest of the mountain and terminates at Alpēnus, the first Locrian town beyond the Malo-Locrian frontier, or (more precisely) at "Melampygus's Rock" and "Cercōpes' Thrones," which is actually the narrowest section [of the Thermopylae Pass]. [AUTHOR.]

[3] The lower pass [of Thermopylae] was held by the forces which I have mentioned, while the mountain path was held by Phocian volunteers who had undertaken this duty for Leonidas. [AUTHOR.]

arrived upon the scene. Seeing troops putting on their equipment, they were taken aback. They had expected to encounter no obstacles and now they had collided with a military force. At this critical moment Hydarnes, who was in terror lest the Phocians might prove to be Lacedaemonians, asked Epialtas the nationality of the force opposing him and, when he learnt the truth, he proceeded to deploy his troops for action. The Phocians no sooner came within range of the heavy and concentrated discharge of the Persian small arms than they turned and fled to the peak of the mountain. They assumed that they were the objective of the attacking force and made up their minds that their last hour had come. While the Phocians were under this impression, however, the Persians with Epialtas and Hydarnes ignored them completely and started to descend the mountain as fast as they could march.

The Hellenes at Thermopylae received the first intimation of the death which awaited them at dawn from the diviner Megistias, after an inspection of the sacrificial victims, and this was confirmed by the news, brought in by deserters, that the Persians were turning their flank. The deserters brought their information before the night was over, and a third alarm was given by the outposts who came running down from the heights at the first streak of day. Thereupon the Hellenes called a council of war in which opinions were divided—one party protesting against any idea of deserting their posts, while the other party pulled the opposite way. Finally the council broke up. Some contingents took their departure, dispersed, and headed for their respective countries, while others had made up their minds to hold their ground and not to desert Leonidas. According to another version, Leonidas took the initiative in dismissing them out of concern to save their lives, although he felt that he personally and the Spartans under his command could not honorably abandon the position which they had originally been sent to hold. This is the view to which I am most inclined to subscribe—namely, that when Leonidas realized that the Allies were half-hearted and unwilling to follow him in persevering to the end, he told them to take their departure, while intimating that he could not himself retire with honor. In holding his ground, he had the prospect of leaving a glorious name behind him without any danger of Sparta's prosperity being obliterated. The Spartans had consulted the Oracle at Delphi regarding the war with Xerxes at the first symptoms of the coming storm, and had received from the Priestess the response that Lacedaemon would be overthrown by the Orientals unless her king lost his life. This response was delivered in the following lines of hexameter verse:

Ye habitants of Sparta's broad domain,
Your city shall by men of Persian strain
Be sacked and lose her glory, or, instead,
Shall mourn a king of saintly lineage dead.

The foe—nor strength of bull nor strength of lion [1]
Shall stay him, front to front. He is the scion
Of Zeus, whose strength is his, nor shall be stayed
Until or king or town hath been in ruins laid.

The effect of this response upon the mind of Leonidas and
his desire to monopolize the lasting glory of the occasion for
the Spartans were in my opinion the motives which induced
him to dismiss the Allies, as a preferable alternative to the
disorderly form of withdrawal which must otherwise have been
the consequence of their divided counsels. In this connection,
it seems to me an important piece of evidence that the diviner [2]
attached to the expedition, who has been mentioned as having
foretold the outcome by inspection of the sacrificial victims,
was indisputably urged by Leonidas to retire, in order that he
might not share the Spartans' fate.[3] Accordingly, the Allies,
thus dismissed, took Leonidas's advice and went their ways,
the only contingents that remained on the spot with the Lacedaemonians being the Thespians and Thebans. Of these, the
Thebans remained involuntarily and not of their own free will
(being retained by Leonidas as virtual hostages), while the
Thespians remained as deliberate volunteers. Refusing to take
their departure and to abandon Leonidas and his companions,
they remained on the spot to die with them, under their commander Damophilus, son of Diadromeus.

At sunrise, Xerxes made an offering and then waited for an
interval—approximately until the busy time of the morning[4]
—before launching his attack. These had been the instructions
given by Epialtas, since the descent from the mountain is
more expeditious and the ground to be covered very much
less in extent than the circuitous approach and ascent. When
the Orientals on Xerxes's side eventually advanced, the
Hellenes with Leonidas changed their tactics, in the knowledge that they were going to meet their deaths, and this time
sallied far farther out into the broader part of the neck of
lowland than they had done previously. During the preceding
days the fortified position had been held and they had confined their operations to making sorties into the narrows. On
the present occasion the Orientals found themselves engaged

---

[1] A play upon the name "Leonidas." [ED.]
[2] Megistias the Acarnanian, a reputed descendant of Melampus. [AUTHOR.]
[3] When urged in this fashion, Megistias refused to retire himself, but sent to the
rear his son, who was serving with him and was his only [male] issue. [AUTHOR.]
[4] Literally: "Until the time when the market place fills up" [with people doing
business]. The phrase is drawn from town and not from country life. [ED.]

outside the pass and suffered correspondingly heavy casualties; for the commanders of the respective units were provided with whips, with which they belabored the individual soldiers in their unflagging efforts to drive them toward the front. Many of their troops met their death by being forced into the sea and drowned, while a far larger number still were trampled to death by their comrades, until the losses were past counting. The Hellenes, aware of the death awaiting them at the hands of the enemy forces who were turning the mountain on their flank, were putting forth their utmost strength against the Orientals with the recklessness of doomed men. By that time the majority of them had had their spears broken and they were slaughtering the Persians with their swords. In this phase of the action Leonidas fell after showing the utmost gallantry, as well as other distinguished Spartans.[1] On the same occasion, many distinguished Persians fell likewise, including two sons of Darius, Abrokomes and Hyperanthes, who were born to the king by Phratagun, daughter of Artanes.[2] Thus two brothers of Xerxes were killed in action on this spot, while the body of Leonidas was the object of a violent struggle between the Persians and the Lacedaemonians, which ended in the Hellenes rescuing the body and four times routing their opponents in virtue of their superior valor. This action lasted until the appearance upon the scene of the force with Epialtas; but as soon as the Hellenes learnt of their arrival, the conflict entered upon a final phase of a different character. The Hellenes retreated to the narrow section of the road in their rear, passed the line of the fortifications, and took up their position on the eminence [3] in a single solid body—with the isolated exception of the Thebans. In this position they defended themselves with their knives (if they still had knives to fight with) or otherwise with their hands and teeth until they were buried by the Orientals under a rain of missiles proceeding partly from troops which had followed up their line of retreat and had disorganized the fortifications and partly from others which had made a detour and had hemmed them in from every direction.

Among these heroic Lacedaemonians and Thespians, the greatest hero of all is said to have been the Spartan Diäneces. Before they made contact with the Medes, Dianeces is reported to have delivered himself of an epigram, upon being informed by a Trachinian that when the Orientals discharged their small

---

[1] I have been so much impressed with their valor that I have ascertained their names, as I have likewise done in the case of all the Three Hundred. [AUTHOR.]

[2] Brother of King Darius and son of Hystaspes, son of Arsames. When Artanes gave his daughter in marriage to Darius, he simultaneously gave his whole estate as her dowry, since she was his only child. [AUTHOR.]

[3] At the entrance to the pass, where the marble lion has since been erected over the grave of Leonidas. [AUTHOR.]

arms the sun was hidden by the vast quantity of the missiles—
so great were the enemy's numbers. Far from being dismayed
at this intelligence, Dianeces (so the story goes) evinced his
contempt for the numbers of the Medes by declaring that the
gentleman from Trachis was bringing them excellent news if
the Medes were going to be so obliging as to hide the sun in
order that the Hellenes might be able to fight them in the
shade and not in the glare. This is not the only epigram of its
kind which Dianeces the Lacedaemonian is reported to have
left behind him as a memorial. Next to Dianeces, two Lacedaemonian brothers, Alpheus and Maron, sons of Orsiphantus,
are said to have distinguished themselves most conspicuously,
while the Thespian who best acquitted himself was one named
Dithyrambus, son of Harmatidas. They are buried on the
actual spot where they fell, and, with them, the other Hellenes
killed in action before the departure of the contingents dismissed by Leonidas. Upon the monument there is engraved
the following inscription:

> Against three million battled here of yore
> From Pelops's Island thousands four.

This is the inscription on the common monument, while the
Lacedaemonians have a special epitaph as well:

> Go, friend, tell Lacedaemon: In this land
> We lie, obeying her command.

That is the Lacedaemonians' epitaph, and the following is the
diviner's:

> Here lies Megistias, whom Median quiver
> Slew, when Medes passed Spercheus's river.
> Diviner he, death's angels found him fey,
> Yet scorned he Sparta to betray.

These epitaphs, and the monuments on which they are inscribed, are all tributes from the Amphictyonic League, except
for the epitaph on the diviner Megistias, which was inscribed
by Simonides, son of Leoprepes, in token of personal friendship.

There is a story that two of the Three Hundred Spartans,
Eurytus and Aristodamus, were both presented with the possibility (had they acted in concert) of returning safely home to
Sparta together—considering that they had been given leave
from the front by Leonidas and were in hospital at Alpeni
with acute ophthalmia—unless they preferred the alternative
of losing their lives with their comrades. When this choice

was presented to them, they could not make up their minds
to agree, but took different views of their duty. Eurytus had
no sooner ascertained that the Persians were turning the army's
flank than he asked for his equipment, put it on and ordered
his servant to guide him to the scene of action. The servant
did so, but having done so he turned and fled, whereupon
Eurytus flung himself into the melee and met his death. Aristodamus, on the other hand, found his courage failed him and
he stayed behind. Now supposing that Aristodamus, when he
came home, had been the only case in hospital, or supposing
that the two of them had come safely back together, it is my
belief that the Spartans would not have visited them with their
resentment. The fact, however, that one of them had actually
met his death, while the other, who had the same excuse
(neither better nor worse) to cling to, had not made up his
mind to lose his life, compelled the Spartans to be implacable
in visiting their resentment upon Aristodamus.[1] After returning to Lacedaemon, Aristodamus was received with insult and
contumely. The contumely took the practical form that no
Spartan would give him a light for his fire or speak to him,
while he was insulted with the nickname of "Runaway Aristodamus." At the battle of Plataea, however, he made good all
the imputations upon his character.[2] There is also said to have
been another survivor of these Three Hundred named Pan-
tītes, who had been sent with dispatches to Thessaly and who
returned to Sparta, was treated with contumely and committed
suicide.

[1] While, according to one version, Aristodamus came safely back to Sparta in the
circumstances and upon the excuse that I have mentioned, there is another version
to the effect that he had been sent to the rear with dispatches but could have
managed, had he chosen, to return in time to take part in the action—instead of
which, he saved his life by dawdling on the road, whereas his fellow dispatch-
bearer reached the scene of action and lost his life. [AUTHOR.]

[2] Book IX, chapter 71: At the battle of Plataea, the Spartan who showed by
far the greatest gallantry was (in my judgment) Aristodamus, who had been
treated with insult and contumely for being the only one of the Three Hundred
to come back safe from Thermopylae. Next to him, the Spartans Posidonius,
Philocyon, and Amompharētus distinguished themselves most conspicuously. On
the other hand, in a discussion as to which of them had shown the greatest gallantry, the Spartans present came to the conclusion that the prodigies of valor
accomplished by Aristodamus, who behaved like a man possessed and would not
keep his place in the ranks, were inspired by his unconcealed wish to die on
account of the imputation under which he labored, while Posidonius had fought
like a hero without any desire to lose his life—a factor which, in their judgment,
gave the measure of Posidonius's superiority. This pronouncement might conceivably have been dictated by envy; but the fact remains that all the individuals
whom I have mentioned who fell in this battle, with the exception of Aristodamus,
were awarded honors, while Aristodamus, who wished to die on account of the
imputation aforementioned, received none. [AUTHOR.]

ATHENS
(431 B.C.)
(THUCYDIDES OF ATHENS: Book II, chapters 34–46)

THE same winter, the Athenians observed an ancestral custom
by giving a public funeral to those who had fallen in the first
campaign of the war. The procedure is that the remains of the
dead should lie in state before the ceremony for three days,
during which the relatives have an opportunity to pay their
tribute. The procession itself consists of hearses bearing cy-
presswood coffins, one for each battalion,[1] in which the remains of that battalion's dead are assembled, while a single
bier, draped but empty, commemorates the missing. Anyone,
Athenian or alien, is at liberty to follow, and the female relatives of the dead attend to wail at the tomb. They are interred
in the national mausoleum, in the most beautiful suburb of
the town, which is the regular burial place for those who die
on the field of honor, except the dead of Marathon, whose
gallantry was felt to be so conspicuous that they were buried
where they fell. When the grave has been filled, a speaker
chosen by the state for his distinction of intellect and character delivers a fitting panegyric and then the mourners disperse.
That is the ceremonial, and, throughout the war, the custom
was observed when occasion arose. On this first occasion the
choice fell upon Pericles, son of Xanthippus; and, when the
moment arrived, he came forward from the monument,
mounted an elevated platform which had been constructed for
the occasion in order that his voice might carry to the greatest
possible distance, and delivered himself as follows:

"It has been the practice of my predecessors to commend
the statesman who added this address to the customary procedure. It is right, they tell us, that such an address should be
delivered at the burial of those who have fallen on the field
of honor. For my own part, I am inclined to think that those
who have proved their worth by their deeds would be sufficiently honored by receiving their tribute in the same kind—
such a tribute, in fact, as meets your eyes in this public
ceremonial—that it would be wiser not to intrust the reputations of so many brave men to the uncertain talents of a single
speaker. It is by no means easy for a speaker to do justice to a
theme when it is difficult to convince the audience that he is
speaking the truth. The friends of the dead who know their

[1] There were only ten battalions in the Athenian citizen-army. [ED.]

37

story will probably feel his words inadequate both in form and substance, while strangers, out of jealousy, will suspect a certain exaggeration, if the qualities attributed to the dead surpass their own. The truth is that the eulogy of others is only tolerable so long as the hearers feel that they could each have risen to the occasion had the part fallen to them. They begrudge and therefore refuse to believe whatever is beyond their range. It has been decided, however, by our predecessors that this is what should be; and so I must defer to the custom in my turn and must do my best to satisfy the different views and feelings of my audience.

"I shall begin with our ancestors, for this is an occasion on which a tribute to their memory is both due and proper. This country has ever been inhabited by the same race, whose valor has bequeathed it as a home of freedom from one generation to another down to this day. All honor to our forefathers and, above all, to our own fathers, who by their labors added to their heritage and handed on to ourselves the great empire which we now possess. The boundaries of that empire have been extended in almost every quarter by many of those present who are not yet past the prime of life, and the resources of the commonwealth have been developed by our efforts to the maximum of self-sufficiency, for peace or for war. The military achievements by which our possessions were successively acquired, and the vigor displayed by our fathers and ourselves in repelling the aggressions of our enemies, Oriental or Hellenic, are too familiar for me to weary you with their recital; but I shall attempt to describe the institutions which have won us our position and the qualities inherent in our public and private life to which it owes its greatness, before proceeding to perform my duty toward those who lie here, because I believe that this theme is proper to the occasion and edifying to my audience, including the strangers in our midst.

"The constitution under which we live seeks no inspiration from abroad, and so far from being borrowed it has been taken as an example. The possession of the franchise by a majority instead of a minority has earned for it the title of Democracy. Before the law, equality is assured to every citizen in his dealings with his neighbor; the recognition of personal distinction in any field and the political advancement which is its reward are determined by merit and not by social standing; and no stigma attaches to poverty which can bar the career of any man capable of serving the state. We lead a life of freedom not only in our politics but in our mutual tolerance of private conduct. We do not resent our neighbor doing what he pleases, nor subject him to those marks of disapproval which poison pleasure though they may inflict no formal injury; and while our private intercourse is thus free from constraint, this does not react to the detriment of law and order, which are preserved by a wholesome respect for the constituted authorities and for the laws of the land, especially those which protect the victims of injustice and those whose moral sanction is so strong that there is no need for them to be written.

"We have understood how to vary work with recreation by an annual succession of civic and religious festivals and by the refinement of our homes, the daily delight of which assists us to banish care. The size of our city attracts imports from every part of the world, and the products of our own country are not more thoroughly ours to enjoy than those of other climes.

"We also differ in our military institutions from our opponents. We throw our country open to all mankind, and never resort to aliens' acts in order to conceal information which might possibly assist the enemy if it fell into his hands. We prefer to rely upon our valor in the field and not upon secret military preparations. In education, again, we leave it to our opponents to cultivate manliness by a laborious training from their tender years upward, while we, with our undisciplined life, are as ready as they to face every reasonable danger. This is proved by the facts. The Lacedaemonians never invade our country alone, but with the combined forces of their confederacy, whereas, when we attack our neighbors, we seldom find difficulty in defeating them, though we are the invaders and they are defending their homes. Again, our united forces have never yet been faced by any opponent, because we are continually dispersing them on expeditions by land, in addition to the requirements of our fleet. Yet whenever they encounter a fraction of our forces and defeat them, they boast that they have been victorious against our total strength, while, if they are worsted, they maintain that it has taken our total strength to secure the victory. However that may be, the fact that we preserve a military spirit by a life of ease instead of deliberate hardship and by a natural rather than an artificial courage gives us a double advantage. We are not compelled to anticipate the rigors of war, yet we face them, when they come, as courageously as those who are in perpetual training.

"But these are not our country's only claims to admiration. Besides all this, we cultivate the arts without extravagance and the intellect without effeminacy. We care more for the uses of wealth than for its show, and see the real disgrace of poverty not in admission of the fact but in neglect to seek a remedy. Our politicians do not neglect their private affairs, and the rest of us devote ourselves to business without losing touch with politics. We are unique in regarding men who take no part in politics as not merely unambitious but unprofitable; and we are all sound judges, if not creative statesmen, in public affairs. In our belief, action suffers not from discussion but from lack of discussion to enlighten it before it is taken; and we combine to an exceptional degree the qualities of daring and deliberation, whereas in most natures courage is the fruit of stupidity and hesitation the penalty of reflection. Yet the finest characters are surely those which realize the most clearly where pleasure and pain await them, yet are not deterred by their knowledge from facing the worst. We are equally exceptional in our moral standards, for we make our friends by performing and not by receiving services; and the party which confers the obligation is of course the firmer friend of the two, in his efforts to keep the recipient in his debt by continued kindness, while the debtor's feelings are blunted by the knowledge that any return he makes will be not a favor but an obligation. We alone are inspired by the spirit of freedom to put self-interest aside and to do good regardless of the consequences.

"In short, I maintain that the Commonwealth of Athens is the School of Hellas and that the individual Athenian will never meet his equal for self-reliance, versatility, and gallantry in whatever situation he may find himself. The proof that this is no empty boast but sober reality is afforded by the power of our country, which is the fruit of our national character. Athens alone of her contemporaries more than justifies her promise by her performance; she alone is a power by whom it is no dishonor to her enemies to be worsted and no grievance to her subjects to be ruled. Nor will our power pass without a memorial. The proofs by which we have signalized it insure us the admiration of our contemporaries and of all posterity. We need no Homer to praise us nor other poet to clothe our achievements with the ephemeral glamor that wilts under the light of truth. Our daring has forced an entrance into every sea and every land, and everywhere we have raised imperishable monuments of our presence for good or for evil.

"Such is the country in whose cause these dead have made their noble choice. Rather than be bereft of her, they died on the field of honor, and the least that we who survive them can do is to spend ourselves, one and all, in her service. If I have enlarged upon her genius, my purpose has been to show you that we possess a greater treasure to fight for than those who can boast of no similar inheritance, and to place my eulogy of the heroes whom I am privileged to commemorate upon an uncontrovertible foundation. The substance of that foundation has been laid already, for the Athens which I have praised is what the heroism of these and others like them has made her —men whose fame, almost alone in all Hellas, is only commensurate with their deserts. They have all died a soldier's death, whether that death gave the first glimpse of the spirit that was in them or set the seal upon it. Valor in the field in defense of home and country covers a multitude of sins. Such public service outweighs many disservices in private life and enables those who render it to redeem their characters. Among these dead there were both rich and poor; yet the rich were not unnerved by the temptation to prolong the enjoyment of their wealth, nor the poor induced to postpone the risk of death by the prospect of even yet exchanging poverty for ease. In their eagerness to strike a blow at their enemies they rose superior to such motives; they held this risk to be the noblest that a man can take; and they took it deliberately, in order to strike their blow, though without abandoning their other aspirations. Committing the uncertain chances of success into the keeping of Hope, they trusted in nothing but their own right hands to accomplish the work that lay before them. They felt that to lose their lives in action was to save them in a truer sense than to save them by giving way, and so they turned their backs on moral disgrace and stood their ground in physical combat, until the swift stroke of Fate released them from this mortal life in an ecstasy not of fear but of glory.

"Thus these dead acquitted themselves as became Athenians, and it is for us who survive them to see that we face the foe with a resolution as unfaltering as theirs, though we may legitimately pray to be spared their fate. You know what are the rewards of valor as well as the most prolix speaker could expound them to you; but, instead of envisaging them in the abstract, you are privileged to contemplate day by day the manifestations of our country's power. Be her lovers, and, when her greatness fills your understanding, realize that it is the achievement of men—men who dared for her and planned for her and faced death for her, and who never felt that failure in an enterprise was a reason for depriving their country of their valor, the noblest offering that they could lay at her feet. They gave their lives to their country and won immortal praise for themselves—immortal praise and the noblest of all sepulchers, not merely the sepulcher in which their bodies lie, but that in which their glory is enshrined at all times, for word or deed to recall it, world without end. The sepulcher of heroes is the whole earth, and epitaphs inscribed in the land of their birth are not the only monuments that mark it. In lands which they never knew they possess monuments not graven on stone but implanted in the hearts of all men.

"Take them as your ensamples; learn from them that happiness consists in freedom and freedom in valor; and never stand aside from the perils of war. The unfortunate, with no prospect

of success before them, who are generally expected to be reckless of their lives, have less call to be so than those whose
career is still exposed to the risk of a change for the worse
and who have therefore most to lose by a catastrophe. To men
with souls the degradation of cowardice is something more
painful than an instantaneous· death in the glory of their
strength and patriotism.

"There is a lesson in this for the parents, here present, of the
dead, to whom I now address myself with a message of con-
solation rather than condolence. They realize the changes and
chances of this mortal life—a life in which true success is to be
found in some end as glorious as that achieved by their children (whatever sorrow it may entail for themselves) and in an
existence in which happiness is coextensive with life itself. I
know well that this is a hard saying; that the happiness of
others—such happiness as once rejoiced your own hearts—
will often remind you of your loss; and that what wounds is
not the absence of blessings outside our experience but the
withdrawal of blessings grown familiar to us by use. But your
duty is endurance—tempered by the hope of other children,
in the case of those who are still of an age to have them. These
babes yet unborn, with whom some of you will be blessed,
will efface from the hearts of their parents the memory of
those that are not, and will banish the specters of depopulation and insecurity from the country. Citizens who have not
children to give as hostages to Fortune can never play so fair
or just a part in politics as their fellows. As for those of you
who are too old to replace their loss, they must console themselves with the happiness that has attended the longer portion
of their lives and with the comparative brevity of the remainder, and must find relief for their own pain in their children's
glory. Nothing is immortal but the spirit of honor, and the
true alleviation of the lean years is not to have made a fortune,
as some would have it, but to have earned the esteem of
others. Turning to the sons and brothers, here present, of the
dead, I foresee that they have a formidable task before them.
No one has anything but praise for the departed; and even if
you do wonders, you will be fortunate if you are regarded not
as their equals but as barely their inferiors. The living have
always jealousy to contend with, while those no longer in our
path are honored with an affection unqualified by rivalry.
There are also new-made widows among you, on whose account I must not pass over the duties of women; but one
sentence will convey the sum of the matter. Your highest
ambition should be not to fall below the level on which you
have been placed by nature, and to be as little heard of as
possible, for good or evil, among the other sex.

"The task imposed upon me by custom is now accomplished to the best of my ability. My words are said, and these dead have received the material honors due to their mortal remains. The country has still to honor them by educating their children at the public expense until they come of age. This honor, which commences from today, is the prize which Athens offers to these heroes and to their survivors in the race which they have run; and what prize could be better? For where the rewards of valor are, there will valiant men be gathered together. . . .

"And now, bewail your dead and go your ways."

This was the address with which the funeral of the fallen was celebrated that winter, which concluded the first year of the war.

LIBERTE—EGALITE—FRATERNITE
(*ca.* 431–425 B.C.)

(Anon.=Pseudo-Xenophon: *Institutions of Athens:* chapter I, [10-12])

SLAVES, again, and permanently domiciled aliens enjoy an extreme degree of license at Athens, where it is illegal to assault them and where the slave will not make way for you. The reason why this is the local custom shall be explained. If it were legal for the slave to be struck by the free citizen, or for the alien or for the freedman, it would often have occurred that somebody should strike the Athenian citizen through mistaking him for a slave. The free proletariat at Athens are no better dressed than the slaves and aliens and no more respectable in appearance. If any reader is surprised at the further fact that at Athens they allow the slaves to live in luxury and in some instances to keep up an imposing establishment, it would not be difficult to indicate the wisdom of their policy on this point as well. The fact is that, wherever naval power exists, it is essential for slaves to bring in money by their services, in order that I [the master] may receive at least the royalties upon my slave's labor, and this involves [eventual] manumission. In a country, however, in which wealthy slaves exist, it is no longer desirable that my slave should be afraid of you—as would, in fact, be the case in Lacedaemon. If your slave is afraid of me, he will be always consequently in danger of having to give up his own money in order to escape danger to his own person. This is the reason why we have extended the benefits of Democracy to the relations between slaves and freemen and between aliens and citizens—the explanation being that the country requires the permanent residence of aliens in her midst on account both of the multiplicity of trades and of her maritime activities. On this account we have very sensibly extended the benefits of Democracy to the aliens as well.

THE CLASS WAR: FIRST PHASE
(427–425 B.C.)

(THUCYDIDES: Book III, chapters 70–85, and Book IV, chapters 46–48)

THE civil disorders in Corcyra began with the return of the prisoners taken in the naval battles off Epidamnus,[1] who had been liberated by the Corinthians—nominally on the security of 800 talents deposited by their representatives,[2] but actually in consideration of the fact that they had agreed to bring Corcyra over into the Corinthian camp. These ex-prisoners duly started to intrigue, by canvassing their fellow-citizens individually, with a view to detaching their country from the alliance with Athens. Upon the arrival of an Athenian and a Corinthian vessel, both bringing diplomatic missions, the Corcyraeans, after negotiation, formally resolved to observe their treaty obligations by remaining in alliance with Athens, without prejudice to the friendly relations already existing between them and the Peloponnesians. The conspirators' next step was to bring an action against Pīthias (honorary representative of Athens and leader of the proletariat in Corcyra) on the charge that he was forcing Corcyra into subservience to Athens. Pithias was acquitted and proceeded to bring a counter-action against the five wealthiest members of the group on the pretext that they had been cutting stakes in the grove consecrated to Zeus and Alcinous[3]—the penalty prescribed for each stake being one gold piece. The defendants lost their case and took sanctuary at the shrines owing to the heaviness of the fine, in the hope of being allowed to pay it by instalments, whereupon Pithias, who also happened to be a member of the Council, prevailed upon that body to put the law into effect. At this the conspirators, rendered desperate by the law and also hearing

[1] In 436-2 B.C. Epidamnus is the modern Durazzo. [ED.]
[2] In Greek πρόξενον or persons who acted on behalf of aliens—a technical term to which there is hardly an equivalent in English, since the πρόξενος was a distinguished private citizen of the country in which he acted (like some modern vice-consuls) and not an official of the foreign state on behalf of whose nationals he acted (like the regular members of our own consular service). [ED.]
[3] King of the legendary Phaeacians in the *Odyssey* and a patron saint or hero of Corcyra, which the Hellenic colonists identified with the Phaeacians' island of Scheria. [ED.]

that Pithias, before ceasing to be a member of the Council, intended to persuade the masses into concluding an offensive and defensive alliance with Athens, banded together, armed themselves with daggers, burst into the Council and assassinated not only Pithias but no less than sixty other persons, including councilors as well as private individuals, while a few isolated supporters of Pithias's policy made their escape to the Athenian warship, which was still in harbor. The assassins called an assembly of the citizen-body, in which they declared that what had happened was all for the best and would incidentally save them from falling into subservience to Athens. For the future they proposed that they should admit neither party unless they came with a single ship at a time on peaceful errands, and that they should treat any larger force as an enemy. These declarations they compelled the assembly to confirm forthwith in a motion, and they at once sent a mission to Athens to justify what had been done and to dissuade the refugees there from any hostile measures which might lead to a reaction. Upon their arrival, the Athenians arrested the mission as revolutionaries, as well as anyone who listened to them, and interned them in Aegina.

Meanwhile, the party in power at Corcyra took advantage of the arrival of a Corinthian warship with a Lacedaemonian diplomatic mission to attack the proletariat and to defeat them in a regular battle. When night descended, the proletariat took refuge in the citadel and the high-lying parts of the town and concentrated their forces upon establishing themselves in that position, in addition to holding the Hyllaïc harbor, while the other party occupied the *piazza*, where most of them lived, and the adjoining harbor facing the Continent. Next day they indulged in a little outpost fighting and both sent emissaries round the countryside inviting the slaves to join them and promising them their liberty. The proletariat were joined by the majority of the slaves, while the other party were reinforced by 800 mercenaries from the Continent. After a day's inaction, fighting started again, and this time victory was secured by the proletariat, who possessed the superiority in position and numbers. Their women also gave them courageous support by pelting the enemy with tiles from the houses and facing the uproar and commotion with a steadfastness unusual in their sex. The decision was reached late in the evening, when the reactionaries—in a panic lest the proletariat should rush the dockyard and annihilate them—set fire to the houses and tenements surrounding the *piazza*, without sparing either their own property or their neighbors', with the consequence that a vast quantity of merchants' stocks was consumed, while the entire town was in danger of destruction if the flames had

been fanned by a wind blowing in that direction. At this point
the action ceased and both sides passed the night inactive but
on the alert. The Corinthian ship found it advisable, after the
victory of the proletariat, to steal out to sea, while the majority
of the mercenaries deserted and made their way across to the
Continent. On the following day Nicostratus, son of Diï-
trephes, holding the rank of general in the Athenian army,
arrived from Naupactus with twelve ships and five hundred
Messenian infantry to meet eventualities. Nicostratus proceeded to negotiate a settlement, and persuaded the parties to
agree upon bringing ten of the ringleaders (who did not wait
for the sequel) to trial, while the rest were to remain in peace
after entering into an offensive and defensive alliance with
one another and with Athens. After achieving this result, he
was on the point of setting sail when the leaders of the proletariat persuaded him to leave five of his own ships behind
with them to discourage any tendency toward restiveness
among their opponents, while they undertook to replace them
by an equal number of ships with Corcyraean crews. Nicostratus had no sooner consented than the proletarian leaders
began to conscript their enemies for service on the ships
offered. In terror of being sent off to Athens, the conscripts
took sanctuary in the shrine of the Dioscuri. Nicostratus attempted to induce them to quit sanctuary and to reassure them,
but without success—whereupon the proletariat seized the
pretext for mustering in arms, on the ground that sinister intentions were revealed by their adversaries' hesitation to serve
in the squadron. They proceeded to confiscate the arms in the
reactionaries' houses, and, but for the intervention of Nicostratus, they would have butchered individual members of the
party whom they encountered. Seeing what was in progress,
the remainder took sanctuary in the shrine of Hera to the
number of not less than four hundred. It was now the turn of
the proletariat to be terrified lest the suppliants should start a
revolution, and they accordingly persuaded them to quit sanctuary and conveyed them to the island off the shrine, where
they were supplied with provisions. At this stage in the civil
disorders, and four or five days after the conveyance of the
individuals in question to the island, the Peloponnesian
squadron which had been stationed at Cyllene [1] after its return
from Ionia arrived, fifty-three sail strong—still under the
command of Alcidas, but with Brasidas on board as his ad-
viser. After anchoring in the continental harbor of Sybota
they bore down upon Corcyra at dawn. Under stress of the
twofold anxiety occasioned by the situation in the town and

[1] The naval base of the State of Elis in the Peloponnese = the modern Katakolo.
[ED.]

by the naval attack, the proletariat lost their nerve and, while proceeding to clear sixty ships for action, they persisted in launching them piecemeal against the enemy as fast as they were manned, although the Athenians urged them to allow them (the Athenians) to sail out first and to follow themselves with their united forces. When the Corcyraean ships found themselves out of formation in the presence of the enemy, two of them at once deserted, while on board others the crews began to fight among themselves, and there was an utter lack of discipline in all their proceedings. Seeing the disorder, the Peloponnesians told twenty ships to deal with the Corcyraeans and concentrated the rest against the twelve Athenian ships, which included the *Salaminia* and the *Paralus*. The Corcyraeans, who engaged unskillfully and in driblets, found themselves hard pressed in their sector. Meanwhile the Athenians, who were alarmed at the enemy's superiority and at the danger of encirclement, declined to engage the ships detailed against them in a body or at their center, but attacked on the wing and sank one vessel. When the Peloponnesians formed in a circle the Athenians started to sail round them and attempted to upset their formation. The maneuver was noticed by the detachment operating against the Corcyraeans, and these, fearing a repetition of the battle of Naupactus,[1] came to the rescue, whereupon the united squadron bore down upon the Athenians in a body. The Athenians then began to back astern, their object being to secure the longest possible start for the Corcyraeans in their race for shelter, which they could do by backing slowly themselves and drawing off the enemy's forces. After proceeding on these lines, the engagement came to an end at sunset, when the Corcyraeans took fright lest the enemy should bear down upon the town itself in prosecution of their victory and either take on board the prisoners then on the island or effect some other *coup* of the kind. They therefore conveyed the prisoners back from the island to the shrine of Hera and put the town in a state of defense. In spite of their victory, however, the enemy did not venture to attack the town, but sailed back to their anchorage off the Continent with thirteen Corcyraean ships in tow. The next morning, they showed as little inclination as ever to bear down upon the town, although the Corcyraeans were in utter disorder and panic. Brasidas is reported to have urged Alcidas to take this course, but he had not been given an equal voice in the command. Instead, the Peloponnesians made a landing on the promontory of Leucimmē and started to devastate the countryside. Meanwhile, the Corcyraean proletariat had fallen

[1] A victory which the Athenian commander Phormio had gained in 429 B.C. by the same maneuver. [ED.]

into such an extremity of panic lest the enemy fleet should attack that they entered into negotiations with the suppliants and their friends in order to save the town. Some of the reactionaries were actually induced to go on board ship, for they did after all man thirty ships in the expectation of an attack. However, after spending till midday in laying the country waste, the Peloponnesians sailed off, and at nightfall the approach of sixty Athenian ships was signaled to them by beacon. This squadron had been dispatched, under the command of Eurymedon, son of Theocles, by the Athenian Government as soon as they heard of the disorders in Corcyra and of the prospect that Alcidas's squadron would attack the island. At the news, the Peloponnesians immediately started to make their way homeward without waiting for daylight. They hugged the coast, hauled their ships over the Isthmus of Leucas in order not to be detected in the process of sailing round, and made good their retreat. As soon as the Corcyraeans saw the Athenian squadron approaching and found that the enemy squadron had disappeared, they sent to bring the Messenians into the town,[1] ordered the ships which they had manned to sail round into the Hyllaïc harbor, and, while they were on their way, they started to massacre any of their enemies upon whom they could lay hands. They proceeded to disembark from the ships the individuals whom they had persuaded to go on board, and to butcher them, after which they went to the shrine of Hera, induced about fifty of the suppliants to stand their trial, and condemned them all to death. The majority of the suppliants, who had not been induced to quit sanctuary, began to make an end of one another there in the shrine. Some hanged themselves on the trees, while others destroyed themselves in various ways as best they could. For the week during which Eurymedon, after his arrival, remained in port with his sixty ships, the Corcyraeans continued to massacre such of their countrymen as they regarded as their enemies. The crime imputed to their victims was that of plotting the overthrow of the proletariat, but there were individuals who met their death in satisfaction of private feuds, while others met it at the hands of their debtors. Death reigned in all its most horrible forms. As is apt to happen in such situations, there was no limit to the lengths to which atrocities were carried. There were cases of fathers massacring their children and of suppliants being dragged from the altars and massacred as they clung to them, while a particular group of victims actually met their death by being immured in the temple of Dionysus.

Such was the savagery with which the class war at Corcyra developed, and it made the deeper impression through being

[1] They had previously been encamped outside. [AUTHOR.]

the first case of its kind, whereas eventually the upheaval spread through practically the entire Hellenic world. In every country there were struggles between the leaders of the proletariat and the reactionaries in their efforts to procure the intervention of the Athenians and the Lacedaemonians respectively. In peacetime they would have had neither the opportunity nor the desire to call in the foreigner; but now there was the war, and it was easy for any revolutionary spirits in either camp to procure an alliance involving the discomfiture of their opponents and a corresponding reinforcement of their own faction. This access of class war brought one calamity after another upon the countries of Hellas—calamities that occur and will continue to occur so long as human nature remains what it is, though they may be aggravated or mitigated or modified by successive changes of circumstance. Under the favorable conditions of peacetime, both countries and individuals display a sweeter reasonableness, because their hands are not forced by the logic of events; but war eats away the margins of ordinary life and, in most characters, adjusts the temperament to the new environment by its brutal training. So the countries of Hellas became infected with the class war, and the sensation made by each successive outbreak had a cumulative effect upon the next. It was a competition of ingenuity in the elaboration of intrigue and in the refinement of reprisals. The customary meaning of words was arbitrarily distorted to cover the conduct of those who employed them. Reckless irresponsibility was treated as courageous loyalty, cautious reserve as cowardice masked under a high-sounding name, restraint as a cloak for poor-spiritedness, and the policy of reason as a policy of *laissez-faire*. A frenzied fanaticism was the popular ideal of conduct, while intrigue that took no risks was regarded as a legitimate method of self-defense. Violence of feeling was a warrant of honesty, deprecation of violence a signal for suspicion. Success in intrigue was the test of intelligence and the detection of intrigue a testimonial to superior cleverness, while anyone who so shaped his policy as to dispense with such methods was pilloried as a nihilist toward his own group and a weakling in face of their opponents. In short, approbation was reserved for those who forestalled their enemies in striking a blow or who implanted that suggestion in minds which had not previously conceived it. The ties of party actually became closer than those of kinship, because partisans were readier than kinsmen to throw themselves into an adventure at a moment's notice, and the associations in question were not formed to secure the benefits of established institutions but to gain illegitimate advantages by violating them. Complicity in crime was a more effective sanction for loyalty to engagements than a solemn oath. A fair offer from opponents was received as a signal for practical precautions by the dominant party of the moment, instead of evoking any generous response. The exaction of reprisals was valued more highly than immunity from wrongs demanding them. The rare covenants of reconciliation were only entered into on either side as a momentary last resort and only observed so long as no alternative resource presented itself. Anyone who spied a weak spot in his adversary's armor and had the nerve to seize his opportunity took more satisfaction in obtaining his revenge by treachery than in fair fight, the dominating considerations being the elimination of risk and the added halo of intellectual brilliance investing the triumphs of perfidy. As a general rule it is easier to obtain the reputation of adroitness by criminality than that of uprightness by stupidity, and human nature is as much ashamed of the one reputation as it rejoices in the other. The cause of this whole phenomenon was the thirst for power arising from the predatory and competitive impulses—impulses which engender conflict, from which passion is engendered in its turn. In all the countries of Hellas, the party leaders invented high-sounding catchwords and posed as the champions of political equality for the masses or of moderate conservatism, in order to make spoils out of the public interest which they served with their lips. In their unscrupulous struggle to gain the upper hand over one another they hesitated at nothing and surpassed themselves in the prosecution of their vendettas. So far from attempting to act within the bounds of moral right and national interest, they recognized no limitations on either side except the caprice of the moment. They did not shrink from bringing themselves into power by verdicts immorally obtained against their opponents, if not by naked force, in order to satiate their momentary rancor. In fact, religion had lost its hold upon either party, and they relied upon their powers of misrepresentation to retrieve their good name whenever they had occasion to perpetrate an invidious action. Meanwhile, the moderate elements in every country were preyed upon by the extremists of both camps, partly for their refusal to take sides and partly out of resentment at the prospect of their survival.

Thus the class war plunged Hellenic society into every kind of moral evil. Straightforwardness, the chief constituent of idealism, was laughed out of existence in the terribly prevalent atmosphere of mutual hostility and suspicion. No argument was sufficiently cogent and no oath sufficiently binding to reconcile opponents. The only consideration that made a universal appeal was the hopeless instability of conditions and the consequent advisability of concentrating upon self-protection and taking nothing on trust. In actual fact, the less able combatants were usually the more successful. Just because they were terrified at their own deficiencies and expected to be ·outwitted and outmaneuvered by the superior intelligence, versatility, and nimbleness of their opponents, they plunged recklessly into action; while the intellectually arrogant, who trusted to their wits to forewarn them and disdained recourse to action where judgment would serve, were more often caught defenseless and brought to destruction.[1]

.   .   .   .   .

Such were the passions displayed by the Corcyraeans at home in this first phase of their internecine struggle, up to the moment when Eurymedon and his Athenians sailed off with their squadron. At a subsequent date the Corcyraean exiles, of whom as many as five hundred had made their escape, obtained possession of forts situated on the Continent, which gave them command of the territories belonging to Corcyra across the Channel, and they made these a base for raiding their countrymen in the island—with such destructive effects that the country was overtaken by a severe famine. They also sent missions to Lacedaemon and Corinth to negotiate for their restoration; but, finding diplomacy ineffective, they eventually got together ships and mercenaries, crossed over to the island with a total force of about six hundred men, burnt their boats in order to leave themselves no loophole except through making themselves masters of the country, and ensconced themselves in the fastness of Mount Istōnē, where they constructed a fort, harried the party in power in the town, and made themselves masters of the country with success.

.   .   .   ⌡   .   .

On their way from Pylos to Sicily with an Athenian squadron, Eurymedon and Sophocles touched at Corcyra[2] and made an expedition, with the Corcyraeans holding the town, against the countrymen of the latter who had established themselves on Mount Istone.[3] The attacking party carried the fort by assault, but the garrison in a body made good their escape to a higher-lying position and there capitulated, on the conditions that they should surrender the mercenaries and should themselves surrender their arms, after which their fate should be decided by the Athenian people. Thereupon they were conveyed under flag of truce by the Athenian commanders to the island of Ptychia, to be held in custody there until their dis-

[1] Chapter 84, which is probably spurious, has been omitted. [ED.]
[2] In the summer of 425 B.C. [ED.]
[3] They had come across after the civil disorders, and at the time in question they were masters of the country and were doing a vast amount of destruction. [AUTHOR.]

patch to Athens, on the understanding that, if any individual were caught attempting to escape, the benefit of the truce would be forfeited by all of them. The leaders of the Corcyraean proletariat were afraid that the Athenians might spare the lives of such prisoners as arrived at Athens, and they therefore resorted to the following stratagem. They worked upon a few individuals among the prisoners in the island by secretly sending friends with instructions first to inform them, with all the appearance of good intentions, that their best course was to effect their escape at the earliest possible opportunity, and secondly to promise on their own part to provide a boat, on the allegation that the Athenian commanders intended to surrender them to the Corcyraean proletariat. The trick worked its effect; the boat was duly procured by the *agents provocateurs;* their victims put out to sea in it and were captured, and this meant the automatic annulment of the truce and the surrender of the whole party to the Corcyraeans. A considerable share of responsibility for this result must be borne by the Athenian commanders, who gave a touch of realism to the allegations and encouraged the authors of the intrigue to put it into execution by their unconcealed dissatisfaction at the prospect that the prisoners would be conveyed to Athens by others than themselves,[1] who would thus secure the credit. The prisoners were now handed over to the Corcyraeans. They confined them in a large building and afterward proceeded to draft them out in batches of twenty at a time. These victims were conducted between two ranks of infantry drawn up on either side. They were chained together and exposed to blows and spear thrusts from the troops in the ranks whenever a soldier caught sight of a personal enemy. Men with whips passed along the line to quicken the pace of those who were advancing too slowly. Sixty men had been led out to their deaths in this fashion before their comrades in the building, who imagined that they were being drafted off in order to be lodged elsewhere, discovered what was happening. When they realized the truth and the horror was revealed to them, they appealed to the Athenians and requested them, if they so desired, to put them to death with their hands, but they refused from that moment onward to quit the building and announced their intention of preventing anybody from entering it to the best of their ability. The Corcyraeans, on their part, had no intention of forcing an entrance by the doors, but they climbed to the top of the building, made an aperture in the roof, and started to pour down a rain of tiles and arrows. The prisoners attempted to shield themselves as best they could, while the majority proceeded to put an end to themselves. They picked

[1] Their own destination being Sicily. [AUTHOR.]

up arrows discharged by their persecutors and thrust them down their throats, or hanged themselves with cords taken from some beds which happened to be stored in the place or with strips torn from their clothes. These scenes of horror continued through the greater part of the night (which descended upon the tragedy) before the victims' own hands or the missiles of their assassins on the roof had completed the execution. With the return of daylight, the corpses were piled in layers upon wagons by the Corcyraeans and carted out of the city, while all the women who had been captured in the fort were sold into slavery. This is how the Corcyraeans from the mountain were exterminated by the proletariat. It was the closing scene of the virulent class war in Corcyra—at least so far as the late war was concerned—since it had virtually wiped one of the contending parties out of existence.

PROFESSIONALISM
(401 B.C.)

(XENOPHON OF ATHENS: *The Expedition of Cyrus*:[1] Book I, chapter 2, [14-18])

THE Queen of Cilicia is said to have begged Cyrus to display his army to her, and with this object he held a review of his Hellenic as well as his Oriental forces in the plain. He ordered the Hellenes to parade in their regular battle formation, it being left to each commander to marshal his own men. They formed four deep, with Meno and his regiment on the right, Clearchus and his on the left, and the other commanders in the center. Cyrus began by inspecting the Orientals, who rode past in column of troops and squadrons, and then proceeded to the Hellenes, along whose front he drove in an open and the Queen in a closed carriage. The troops all paraded in bronze helmets, scarlet tunics, and greaves, and with their shields uncased. After driving from end to end of the line, he stopped his carriage in front of the center and sent his dragoman Pigres to the Hellenic commanders with orders to present arms and advance along the whole front. The commanders communicated the orders to the men, and, when the bugle sounded, they presented arms and stepped out. As their pace quickened, however, and they started to cheer, the men broke into the double of their own accord and bore down upon the

---

[1] Literally: "Cyrus's march into the interior" or "up-country" (Ἀνάβασις). This Cyrus, who was the younger brother of King Artaxerxes II (who reigned from 404 to 359 B.C.), is not to be confused with his ancestor Cyrus the Great, the founder of the Persian Empire. [ED.]

camp—a spectacle which threw the Orientals into such a panic that the Queen took to flight in her carriage and the sutlers abandoned their wares and ran away. By the time that they arrived at the camp, the Hellenes were in fits of laughter. The Queen was amazed at the smartness and discipline of the force, while Cyrus was delighted to see the fear which the Hellenes inspired in the Orientals.

SPARTA
(399 B.C.)

(XENOPHON: *History of Hellenic Affairs*: Book III, chapter 3, 4-11)

AGESILAUS had not been on the throne a year when, in the course of conducting one of the regular sacrifices in his official capacity, he was informed by the diviner that the gods were announcing a conspiracy of the most formidable kind. The King repeated the sacrifice and the diviner pronounced the symptoms more formidable than ever. He repeated it again and the diviner said to him: "Sir, by the indications which I am receiving we might be in the very jaws of the enemy." They set to work to sacrifice to the Averters and the Saviors, and barely attained results sufficiently favorable to justify their stopping.

Within five days of the time by which the sacrifice was over, an informer denounced to the Directory[1] the existence of a conspiracy with Cinadon as the ringleader. Cinadon had a youthful appearance and a determined character, but he was not one of the peers.[2] The Directory asked the informer how he thought that the movement would take place, whereupon he told them that Cinadon had taken him to the edge of the *piazza* and had asked him to count how many Spartiates were to be found there. "And so," said the informer, "I counted the King and the Directors and the Privy Councilors and others, up to about forty, and then asked: 'Why ever did you tell me to count them, Cinadon?'—'Because,' said Cinadon, 'you are to regard these as enemies and all the rest as Allies'—amounting to more than 4000 persons who were in the *piazza* at the moment." He added that Cinadon pointed out to him in the streets one "enemy" here and two there as they passed them, while

---

[1] The supreme executive at Sparta consisted of five directors, except on active service, when one or other of the two kings took command. [ED.]

[2] Even among the Spartan citizens, who were themselves a small minority of the total population of the Lacedaemonian territory, there appear to have been two classes called "Peers" and "Inferiors," of whom the former alone were fully enfranchised. [ED.]

all the rest were "Allies." As for any Spartiates who happened to be visiting their country estates, there was one "enemy"—namely, the master—on each property and many "Allies." When the Directors asked him what he believed the number of the conspirators to be, the informer said that Cinadon had spoken with him on this point, too, and had told him that only a restricted number of trustworthy persons were in the confidence of the ringleaders, but that the latter regarded themselves as being in virtual conspiracy with all the serfs and "New Members"[1] and Inferiors and Dependents;[2] for wherever, among these classes, there was any mention of the Spartiates, there was not a man of them who could conceal the fact that he would be delighted to eat them alive. When, again, the Directors asked the informer: "And from what source did they expect to supply themselves with arms?" he reported Cinadon as saying: "Naturally our organized members are in possession of arms, while, as for the masses"—the informer told how Cinadon had taken him to the Iron Market and pointed out to him quantities of knives, quantities of swords, quantities of spits, quantities of hatchets and axes, and quantities of scythes. He reported Cinadon as declaring that there was a potential weapon in every implement for working the soil or timber or stone, and as adding that the majority of the other trades possessed adequate weapons in their tools—especially against unarmed opponents. When asked, again, at what date the movement was timed to take place, he mentioned that instructions had been given to him to remain in town.

The informer's story impressed the Directors as well-considered and filled them with such consternation that they did not even convene the "Small Assembly" but held consultations here and there with individual members of the Privy Council. The Councilors' decision was to send Cinadon to Aulon[3] with other young men, under instructions to arrest and bring back with them certain citizens of Aulon and certain serfs whose names were entered on the tally.[4] They also instructed them

---

[1] Several thousand serfs had been enlisted for dangerous foreign service during the Peloponnesian War (431-404 B.C.) and had been enfranchised (though not raised to full citizenship) as an inducement to volunteer. After demobilization, some of these "New Members" had been secretly destroyed by the Lacedaemonian Government and others settled in a military colony. The survivors were, not unnaturally, discontented. [Ed.]

[2] Sparta, like many other powerful city-states in the Hellenic world, had deprived the weaker neighboring city-states of their sovereignty and had reduced them to the condition of autonomous dependencies. These "dependents" were, of course, in a far happier position than the serfs, since they were personally free and politically self-governing. On the other hand, they had lost their sovereignty and were subject to military service in the Lacedaemonian army. [Ed.]

[3] A dependency of Sparta in the extreme northwestern corner of the Lacedaemonian territory. [Ed.]

[4] The Lacedaemonian Government had a system of writing confidential correspondence crosswise upon narrow strips of papyrus wound diagonally round rollers of various diameters. A document so written could only be read when rewound round a roller of exactly the right dimensions. [Ed.]

to arrest the woman who was said to be the greatest beauty in Aulon and who usually succeeded in demoralizing Lacedaemonian male visitors of all ages. Cinadon had already performed similar services for the Directory on previous occasions, and now, on this occasion, they gave him the tally upon which were entered the names of the persons to be arrested. Cinadon asked which of the young men he was to take with him, to which the Directory replied: "Go to the senior constable[1] and tell him to send with you any six or seven of his men who happen to be on duty." They had taken care that the constable should know which men to send, and that the latter should know that Cinadon was to be arrested. They further informed Cinadon that they proposed to send three carts, in order that his party might not have to bring their prisoners on foot—their object being to conceal as thoroughly as possible the fact that they were sending the party to deal with a single individual in the person of Cinadon himself. They were unwilling to arrest him in town because they did not know the extent of the conspiracy and were anxious first to learn from Cinadon who his associates were, in order to forestall their escape before they realized that they had been denounced. It was arranged that his captors should detain Cinadon himself after his arrest, extract from him the names of his fellow conspirators, and send a written list of them to the Directory as promptly as possible. The Directory's state of mind is revealed by the fact that they reinforced the party dispatched to Aulon with a division[2] of cavalry. As soon as their man had been secured and a trooper had arrived with the list of names which Cinadon had given, the Government at once proceeded to arrest the diviner Tisamenus[3] and the most important of the others. When Cinadon was brought into the presence of the authorities and subjected to cross-examination, and when he proceeded to confess everything and to give the names of his fellow conspirators, they finally asked him whatever had been his object in starting this movement. His answer was: "In order to be as good as anybody else at Sparta." After this answer, he was pilloried in a wooden collar confining his hands and neck, and was paraded round the town with his associates under lash and goad; and so these conspirators met the fate which they deserved.

ἱππαγρέτης = comes stabuli. [ED.]

[2] Corresponding in numbers to no more than a squadron, or even (perhaps) a troop, in a modern Western army. [ED.]

[3] Probably a grandson of the Eléan diviner Tisamenus, son of Antiochus, who had obtained the rare privilege of being naturalized as a Spartan citizen and had won five battles for Sparta between the years 479 and 457 B.C. (Herodotus, IX, 33-36.) [ED.]

SPARTA
(*ca.* 243-240 B.C.)

(PLUTARCH OF CHAERONEA: *Parallel Lives*: Teubner text, ed.
by C. Sintenis, Vol. IV: *Agis*: chapters 5-9 and 18-20)

THE date at which Lacedaemon was first attacked by social
disease and corruption practically coincides with the moment[1]
at which she overthrew the Athenian Empire and gorged herself with the precious metals. At the same time, so long as the
orderliness and equality of the Lycurgean Constitution[2] some-
how or other survived, this saved the country from the consequences of her false steps in other directions, until the election to the Directory of an influential but headstrong and cross-
grained individual named Epitadeus. Epitadeus was led by a
personal quarrel with his own son to draft a bill[3] making it
legal for the holder of a family property or of an allotment to
give it away during his lifetime, or to bequeath it by will, to
anybody whom he chose. In introducing this law, Epitadeus
was simply indulging a private vendetta; but the acquisitive
instinct inspired his countrymen to approve and ratify[4] his
legislation, to the ruin of the best social organization that they
ever had. Thenceforward, the men of influence threw off all
restraint and began to add field to field by elbowing the next
of kin out of their inheritances. The rapid concentration of
wealth in a few hands impoverished the country as a whole,
and the penalties for this were the loss of a liberal outlook and
the closing of liberal careers, with a corresponding growth of
envy and hostility toward the men of property. Not more than
seven hundred Spartiates survived, and of these perhaps a hundred may have owned land and an allotment, while the remainder were a destitute and disfranchised mob sitting idly by
in the town, without any energy or enthusiasm to throw into
the defense of the country against the foreigner, but with eyes
perpetually on the watch for some opportunity of making a
violent internal revolution.

[1] 404 B.C. [ED.]

[2] Lycurgus had fixed the number of households at a constant figure from one
generation to another. The family allotment was bequeathed from father to
son. [AUTHOR.]

[3] Literally "pact," the technical term employed for the constitution traditionally
ascribed to the legendary legislator Lycurgus, who was regarded as the author of a
"social contract." [ED.]

[4] There is no evidence for determining the exact date, and we merely know that
it must have fallen sometime during the first three quarters of the fourth century
B.C., between the close of the Peloponnesian War and the publication of Aristotle's
Politics. (Aristotle mentions this law, but ascribes it to Lycurgus.) We do not
even know whether the law was passed before or after the liberation (in 370 B.C.)
of Messenia, in which many if not most of the Spartan allotments were situated.
[ED.]

This spectacle inspired Agis[1] with the admirable ideal of removing inequalities and supplementing the numbers of the citizen body, and he began to sound people on the question. The younger generation listened to him more quickly than he could have dared to hope and joined him in stripping for the ordeal of honor and in changing their standard of living, like a suit of clothes, for the sake of liberty. The older generation, on the other hand, were so far gone in corruption that most of them were actually filled with fear and trembling at the thought of Lycurgus, like runaway slaves when haled before their master. They were therefore inclined to criticize Agis for deploring the existing situation and regretting the disappearance of the ancient glory of Sparta. However, Lysander, son of Libys and Mandroclīdas, son of Ecphānes, as well as Agesilaus, not only welcomed but stimulated his lofty ambition. Lysander was the most distinguished citizen of Sparta, while Mandroclidas was the cleverest practical politician in Hellas, with a dash of daring to season his *rusée* intelligence. Agesilaus was the King's uncle and a good speaker, but predominantly soft and money-loving. Ostensibly, he was swayed by the encouragement of his son Hippomēdon, who had made his mark as a soldier in many campaigns and was a power in the country in virtue of his popularity with the younger generation; but the genuine motive which induced Agesilaus to participate in the movement was the quantity of his debts, from which he hoped to disembarrass himself by bringing about a revolution. Agis had no sooner secured Agesilaus's adherence than he set to work with his help to win over his mother,[2] whose brother Agesilaus was and whose numerous protégés, friends, and debtors gave her great power in the state and a considerable share in the shaping of policy.

At the first hearing, the queen mother was appalled and attempted to restrain her child from pursuing objects which in her eyes were neither possible nor profitable, but Agesilaus proceeded to explain how admirable and advantageous the policy would be, while the King himself besought his mother to offer up her wealth upon the altar of his glory and ambition. He put it to her that he could not possibly compete in wealth with other sovereigns. The servants of the Pashas and the slaves of the estate-agents of Ptolemy or Seleucus could boast of greater possessions than all the kings of Sparta together; but if he put the luxury of his royal contemporaries in the shade by a display of self-control and simplicity and magnanimity and so succeeded in introducing equality and communism among his fellow countrymen, then he would win the prestige and glory

[1] King Agis IV, son of Eudamidas, of the Eurypontid Dynasty. [ED.]
[2] Agesistrata. [ED.]

of a king who was truly great. In the upshot, the women were so much uplifted by the young man's lofty ambition that they changed their views. Carried away by a potent inspiration of idealism, they not only joined in stimulating Agis and in urging him to prompt action, but sent for their male friends in order to canvass them, besides talking to the other women—with the knowledge, presumably, that the Lacedaemonians are always under the thumb of their women, and that they allow them more liberty of interference in public affairs than they allow themselves in their own households. At that epoch, the greater part of the national wealth of Laconia was in female hands—a fact which placed acute difficulties in the path of Agis's policy. The women were recalcitrant, not only because they were being thrown out of a luxurious life which they vulgarly identified with true happiness, but because they saw themselves being shorn of the influence and consideration which they had been reaping from their riches. Accordingly, they had recourse to Leonidas[1] and begged him, as the senior, to restrain Agis and prevent the execution of his policy. Leonidas was only too anxious to support the rich, but his fear of the proletariat, who had set their hearts upon the revolution, prevented him from offering open opposition. Secretly, however, he attempted to injure and even to wreck the policy by canvassing the authorities and libeling Agis, whom he represented as tempting the poor with the property of the rich as a bribe for procuring despotic power, and as proposing his distributions of land and remissions of debts in order to purchase a goodly company of henchmen for himself and not of citizens for Sparta.

However, Agis succeeded in procuring the election of Lysander to the Directory, whereupon he at once proceeded, through his agency, to introduce a bill into the Council, the principal heads of which were the remission of debts to those who owed them and the redistribution of land. The land [in the Eurotas Basin south of a line running] from the ravine [which joins the Eurotas] opposite Pellānā to [Mount] Taygetus [on the west] and to [Mount] Malea,[2] via Sellasia [on the east],[3] was to be made into 4500 allotments, and the land beyond these limits into 15,000.[4] The latter was to be divided among citizens of the dependencies capable of bearing arms, and the land inside the line among the Spartiates themselves. The deficiency of the Spartiates in numbers was to be supple-

---

[1] Agis's colleague, Leonidas II, of the Agiad Dynasty. [ED.]

[2] Probably a synonym for Mount Parnon, which forms the eastern watershed of the Eurotas Basin, and of which the promontory of Malea is the southern extremity. [ED.]

[3] This appears to have been the boundary of the city-state of Sparta herself as distinguished from her autonomous dependencies. [ED.]

[4] Evidently at the expense of the autonomous dependencies. [ED.]

mented by drawing upon dependents and aliens who had enjoyed a liberal education and who were at the same time of
fine physique and of military age. They were to be organized
in fifteen messes[1] varying in strength from four hundred to
two hundred men, and were to live under the same regime as
their ancestors.

Upon the introduction of the bill into the Council, the members were unable to agree, whereupon Lysander convened
an assembly and addressed the citizens himself, while Mandroclīdas and Agesilaus also begged them not to leave the glory
of Sparta lying in the dust for the sake of a tiny minority that
was living in luxury at their expense, but to remember the succession of oracles warning them to beware of the love of
money as a deadly danger to Sparta—especially the oracles
which they had recently received from Pasiphaa.[2] The speakers
declared that these latter oracles from Pasiphaa likewise en-
joined upon the Spartiates that they should all be equals, in
accordance with the law originally laid down by Lycurgus.
Last of all, King Agis rose and delivered a short speech, the
gist of which was that he was making the largest possible contribution to the constitution which he was seeking to establish.
In fact, he was leading the way by nationalizing his own estate,
which ran into a vast extent of arable and pasture land, not
to speak of six hundred talents in specie. He added that his
mother and grandmother and his friends and associates, who
were the wealthiest people in Sparta, were doing the same.

The proletariat was astounded and overjoyed at the young
man's magnanimity, and hailed him as the first king worthy
of Sparta who had arisen for a full three hundred years. Leonidas, on the other hand, at this point threw himself with all
his might into the cause of opposition.

.   .   .   .   .   .

After ejecting the original Directors [of the year] from office
and creating others, Leonidas at once started machinations
against Agis. First of all, he tried to persuade him to leave
sanctuary[3] and to resume his partnership of the throne, on
the assurance that he had been forgiven by his countrymen.
It was realized (he said) that Agis, in his youthful ambition,
had been led away by Agesilaus. Agis, however, suspected
treachery and refused to move from where he was, whereat

---

[1] In earlier times (from the sixth to the fourth century B.C.) the Spartan mess
had probably been a much smaller unit, perhaps about fifteen men strong, two
messes going to each ἐνωμοτία or minimum military formation. [ED.]

[2] The author's note on the oracle of Pasiphaa at Thalamae in Laconia has been
omitted. [ED.]

[3] The opponents of Agis had carried out a successful counter-revolution, and
Agis himself had taken sanctuary in the precincts of Athena of the Bronze
House. [ED.]

Leonidas desisted from his own deceitful and insincere advances and left the field to Amphāres, Dāmochāres and Arcesilaus, who were in the habit of going up to visit Agis. On one occasion, they took him down with them from the sanctuary to bathe and brought him back, safe and sound, after he had enjoyed his bath. They were all his familiar friends, but Amphares had recently borrowed expensive clothes and plate from Agesistrāta[1] and was for this reason intriguing against the King and his female relations, with intent to defraud them of their property. He is said to have been the most pliant tool of Leonidas and to have worked upon the Directory, of which he was a member.

Agis spent all his time within the sanctuary, except for the visits which he was now in the habit of paying, at irregular intervals, to the bath; so they determined to arrest him there, when he was outside the precincts. They lay in wait until he had finished bathing, and then advanced to meet him, shook hands, and walked on with him—talking and joking as they went as they would to a young man with whom they were intimate. The road had a branch leading, at an angle, toward the prison, and, when their walk brought them to that point, Amphares, in his official capacity, laid hands upon Agis, with the words: "I arrest you, Agis, to answer for your political activities before the Directory." At the same moment Damochares, who was tall and physically strong, lassoed him round the neck with his cloak and began to drag him along. Others hustled him from behind according to plan; nobody came to his assistance, owing to the loneliness of the spot; and so they succeeded in throwing him into prison. Leonidas immediately appeared upon the scene with a strong force of mercenaries and surrounded the building outside, while the Directory went in to confront Agis, and, when they had summoned their partisans on the Council to the building on the pretense of holding a trial, they called upon Agis to defend his conduct. The young man laughed at their sarcasm, whereupon Amphares exclaimed that he would soon sing a different tune when he paid the penalty for his impetuosity. Another of the Directors, by way of giving Agis a chance and hinting at a loophole of escape from the indictment, put to him the question whether he had not acted under pressure from Lysander and Agesilaus. Agis replied that he had acted under pressure from nobody, but had taken up the policy of Lycurgus out of admiration for its first author. The same Director then asked him, again, whether he did not repent of his activities. The young man declared that he did not repent of the best action which he had ever taken, even though

[1] Agis's mother. [ED.]

he were to find himself doomed to suffer for it to the uttermost. At that, they condemned him to death and gave orders to the officials to take him to the "Dechas."[1] Damochares saw that the officials did not venture to lay hands on Agis and that the mercenaries in attendance were displaying an equally intense aversion from the duty, from a feeling that it was an outrage against laws human and divine to do violence to the person of a king. After threatening and abusing them to no purpose, Damochares began to drag Agis toward the building with his own hands. By this time a number of people had become aware of the arrest; there was an uproar and a blaze of torches at the gate, and Agis's mother and grandmother, who had arrived, were crying out in supplication that the King of the Spartans should be granted a fair hearing and a fair trial before his fellow citizens. This led the Government to hasten on the execution as fast as possible, for fear lest he might be rescued from their clutches by night, if greater crowds were to arrive on the scene.

While Agis was on his way to the halter, he noticed one of the officials weeping and giving way to his feelings. "Friend," he said, "weep not for me. In meeting so unlawful and so unjust a death, I am superior to my murderers." After these words, he offered his neck to the noose without resistance. Meanwhile, Amphares advanced to the gate, and when Agesistrata fell on her knees before him under the impulse of their old friendship and familiarity, he raised her up with the assurance that no violence should be committed and no irreparable step taken in Agis's case. He told her, if she liked, to go in and see her son herself. Upon her begging that her mother might accompany her, Amphares declared that there was no objection to that. He let both ladies in, ordered the prison gates to be closed again, and then handed his victims over for execution —first Archidamia,[2] who was by this time extremely old and, in growing old, had become an object of reverence to her fellow countrywomen. When all was over with Archidamia, Amphares ordered Agesistrata to go inside. Upon entering, she saw her son lying on the floor and her mother hanging dead from the noose. Thereupon, with her own hands she assisted the officials to lower her mother to the ground, laid out the body by Agis's side, shrouded it, and covered the face. Then she fell upon her son and kissed his forehead, with the words: "My child, it was your wonderful scrupulousness and gentleness and love of your own kind which brought you to your death in this world of ours." Amphares, who had been watch-

---

[1] A building in the prison, in which they strangle to death condemned persons. [AUTHOR.]

[2] Agesistrata's mother and Agis's grandmother. [ED.]

ing the proceedings from the gate and listening to what was being said, now came upon the scene and exclaimed savagely to Agesistrata: "Well, if you hold the same opinions as your son, you shall suffer the same fate." Agesistrata said, as she rose to meet the halter: "One prayer! May this be for the good of Sparta."

CULTURE
(THIRD CENTURY B.C.)

(POLYBIUS OF MEGALOPOLIS: Book IV, chapters 20-21)

THE Arcadian nation as a whole possesses a Hellenic reputation for good character, not only by reason of the hospitality and human kindness evinced in the lives and characters of the people, but especially on account of the national regard for Religion. It is therefore worth discussing, quite briefly, the problem presented by the savagery of the Cynaethians. The Cynaethians are admittedly Arcadians. What accounts for the cruelty and lawlessness by which they were so sharply distinguished, at that epoch, from their fellow Hellenes? In my opinion, the explanation is to be found in the abandonment by the Cynaethians, first and last among the Arcadians, of the admirable institutions devised by our ancestors—with a scientific adaptation to the facts of environment—for all the inhabitants of Arcadia.

The cultivation of music (that is, of genuine music) is beneficial for all human beings, but for Arcadians it is absolutely indispensable. It is a mistake to suppose, with Ephorus,[1] that music has been introduced among Mankind for no better purpose than deception and charlatanism. It is inconceivable that the ancient Cretans and Lacedaemonians did not know what they were about when they substituted the fife and its rhythm for the trumpet as an accompaniment for military evolutions. It is equally inconceivable that the primitive Arcadians were acting blindly when they welcomed the participation of music in all their institutions—and this to such a degree that they made music a compulsory subject in the education not only of children but of youths from puberty to the age of thirty, whereas in other spheres they were extremely puritanical in their habits. I need not enlarge upon the universally recognized and familiar fact that the Arcadians are almost

[1] Who, on this topic, throws off a remark quite unworthy of him, in the general preface to his work. [AUTHOR.]

unique in their musical regulations. In the first place, Arcadian law insists that children shall be taught from infancy to sing the hymns and carols by which the local saints and deities are traditionally honored in the various districts. After that, they learn the oratorios of Philoxenus and Timotheus,[1] which they perform annually with the keenest enthusiasm in the theaters, to the accompaniment of the Dionysiac orchestras.[2] Not only so, but it is their lifelong custom to look for entertainment at social functions much less to professional performers hired for the occasion than to their own musical talents, which they call upon one another to display in turn. In the case of other attainments they attach no stigma to confessions of ignorance, whereas in the case of singing they are neither in a position to deny their possession of the accomplishment in view of the compulsory musical education which they have all received nor to shake off the obligation when they have admitted it, owing to the fact that in Arcadia this is reckoned a disgrace. Furthermore, there are the marches practiced in formation to the accompaniment of the fife and the dances elaborated under the encouragement of public interest and financial support, which are performed annually in the theaters by the young men for their fellow countrymen's pleasure.

In my opinion these institutions were introduced by our predecessors not at all for the promotion of luxuriousness and of purposeless extravagance but with a clear perception in the first place of the fact that every Arcadian was a worker on the land, with the laborious and forbidding life which this fact implies, and in the second place of the austerity of character which Arcadians acquire from the inclemency and gloominess of the weather usually prevalent in their environment, which inevitably exercises an assimilative influence upon all members of the human race.[3] It was the desire to soften and temper our natural willfulness and forbiddingness that moved our predecessors to introduce all the institutions that I have mentioned, as well as the frequent gatherings and festivals which they made customary for men and women alike, the choirs both of girls and of boys, and, in a word, the innumerable monuments of the ingenuity with which they strove to tame and civilize our stubborn spirits by definite habituation.

These institutions were utterly neglected by the Cynaethians, and that though they stood in particular need of such assistance

---

[1] Philoxenus of Cythera (435-380 B.C.) and Timotheus of Miletus (446-357 B.C.) were two of the most celebrated classical composers in the history of Hellenic music. [ED.]

[2] The children enter for the juvenile and the youths for the so-called adult competitions. [AUTHOR.]

[3] This is, in fact, the capital reason for the main differences of character, physique, and pigmentation which distinguish us from one another in our national and other broad differentiations of type. [AUTHOR.]

owing to the fact that the weather and the landscape of their
country are by far the most forbidding in all Arcadia. Instead,
they threw themselves nakedly into their native occupations
and passions and eventually became brutalized to such a degree
that their enormities are without parallel, for scale and persist-
ency, in any country in the entire Hellenic world. The mis-
guidedness of the Cynaethians in this respect and the disgust
aroused by such conduct among their fellow Arcadians are
both attested by the following circumstance. At the time
when the Cynaethians sent a mission to Lacedaemon after per-
petrating the great massacre, they had to pass through a number of Arcadian towns on their route. Every one of these communities at once expelled them officially from its territory,
while the Mantineans actually held a purification service after
their departure and carried sacrificial victims in procession
round the bounds of their town and territory.

The object of the above digression has been first to save the
Arcadian national character from being brought into ill-repute
by a single Arcadian state; secondly, to combat in Arcadian
minds the notion that the intensive cultivation of music in
their country is a purposeless extravagance and the consequent
tendency to neglect this field of activity; and, thirdly, to make
it easier for the Cynaethians, if ever God relents toward them,
to civilize themselves by turning their energies into the channel of education, especially on the musical side. This is their
only chance of curing the savagery which they displayed upon
the occasion in question.

SOLIDARITY

(227 B.C.)

(POLYBIUS: Book V, chapters 88-90)

THE Rhodians had not let slip the opportunities offered by the
earthquake from which their country had suffered a short time
previously. In this earthquake the great Colossus had collapsed,
as well as the major part of their walls and dockyards, yet they
handled the situation with such businesslike ability that, on the
balance, they gained rather than lost by the disaster. The gulf
between the ignorant improvidence and the intelligent manage-
ment of which human nature is capable is indeed profound, not
only in private life but in public affairs, and, while the improvi-
dent derive injury even from their successes, characters of the
opposite stamp actually find a road to improvement through

their setbacks. The Rhodians are a case in point. In their handling of the situation in question, they brought out the scale and cruelty of the disaster, while at the same time preserving a personal dignity and grandeur in the public appeals and the private conferences conducted by their diplomatic missions. In consequence, they worked upon the feelings of the free states, and still more upon those of the sovereigns, to such an extent that donations not only poured in upon them but the donors actually felt grateful to them for accepting them. Hiero and Gelo[1] not only presented 75 talents of silver[2] as a contribution to the supply of oil for persons using the gymnasium, but dedicated silver cauldrons with stands and a number of ewers, as well as 10 talents toward the upkeep of religious ceremonial and 10 more toward the augmentation of the citizen body, in order to bring their donation up to the round sum of 100 talents. They also granted fiscal immunity to Rhodians calling at their ports and presented the Rhodian Government with 50 four-and-a-half foot catapults. Finally, as though these immense gifts were not enough to cover their obligations, they erected statues at Rhodes in the Bazaar, representing the Rhodian nation in the act of being crowned by the Syracusan. The Rhodians also received a promise from King Ptolemy[3] of 300 talents of silver, 1,000,000 *ardebs* of wheat, sufficient shipbuilding timber for the construction of 10 five-oar-power and 10 three-oar-power warships, 600,000 standard feet of squared deal, 1000 talents of copper cash, 3000 talents of tow, 3000 canvas sails, 3000 talents for the restoration of the Colossus, 100 masons and 350 unskilled workers with 14 talents per annum for their maintenance, as well as 20,000,000 *ardebs* of wheat for the festivals and religious ceremonial, not to speak of 20,000 *ardebs* as rations for 10 warships. The greater part of these gifts were delivered on the spot, including a third of the total money contribution. The Rhodians were similarly presented by King Antigonus[4] with 10,000 lengths of timber (ranging from 24 feet to 12) for the supply of rafters, 5000 ten-and-a-half-foot planks, 3000 talents of iron, 1000 talents of refined pitch, 1000 measures of raw pitch, in addition to which he promised 100 talents of silver, while his queen Chryseïs promised 100,000 measures of wheat and 3000 talents of lead. Seleucus, father of Antiochus,[5] made two separate offers: one of fiscal immunity for Rhodians calling at the ports of his kingdom and the other of

---

[1] Despots of Syracuse. Hiero II reigned from 275 to 216 B.C., and Gelo was his son, who predeceased him. [ED.]
[2] Part of this sum was paid down on the spot and the whole amount within a brief interval. [AUTHOR.]
[3] Of Egypt. [ED.]
[4] Of Macedonia. [ED.]
[5] Sovereign of the majority of the former Persian provinces in Southwest Asia. [ED.]

10 five-oar-power warships equipped for action and 2,000,000 measures of wheat, not to speak of 15,000 feet (weighing 1000 talents) of timber, resin, and hair. The example of the leading monarchs was followed by Prusias and Mithridates and the other Asiatic princes of the day, by whom I mean Lysanias, Olympichus, and Limnaeus. As for the free states which came to the assistance of Rhodes to the extent of their ability, no historian would find it easy to produce an exhaustive catalogue of them. These facts elucidate a problem. When we fix our attention upon the origins of Rhodes and the period that has elapsed since the foundation of the Rhodian state, we are lost in astonishment at the vast progress which the Rhodians have made in so short a time in their private as well as their public fortunes. On the other hand, when we consider the felicity of their geographical position and the foreign imports by which their national wealth is supplemented, we feel—so far from being astonished—that their progress has been inferior, if anything, to what it should be.

The object of the above digression has been to signalize first the grandeur of the Rhodians in their conduct of public affairs —for which they are deserving of all praise and admiration— and in the second place the niggardliness of contemporary sovereigns and the beggarliness of the crumbs which now fall to nations and free states from the royal tables. The sovereigns must not acquire a reputation for generosity at a cost of four or five talents, or expect to enjoy the same popularity and respect in the eyes of the Hellenes as their royal predecessors; nor must the free states, with visible examples before their eyes of the munificence of previous donations, be drawn at this stage into the false step of sacrificing really great distinctions and honors for a mess of pottage. It must be their aim to preserve that sense of proportion which is the chief distinguishing mark of Hellenes as contrasted with other members of the human race.

CIVILIZED WARFARE
(197 B.C.)
(POLYBIUS: Book XVIII, chapter 3)

WHEN Phaenias, the General of the Aetolian Confederacy, had finished speaking,[1] he was followed by Alexander surnamed

[1] The occasion was a conference held in Malis before the decisive campaign in the Second Romano-Macedonian War (200-197 B.C.), which was attended by King Philip V of Macedonia on the one side and the Roman commander T. Quinctius Flamininus, accompanied by representatives of the Hellenic allies of Rome, on the other. [ED.]

Isius, who enjoyed a reputation as an able speaker and man of affairs. Alexander complained that Philip was neither making peace sincerely now nor in the habit of making war honorably when war was the order of the day. Just as his method in conferences and conversations was to lay ambushes and watch for opportunities and behave exactly like a belligerent, so in war itself he followed an immoral and extremely dishonorable line of conduct. He abandoned any attempt to face his opponents in the field, but signalized his flight by burning and plundering the towns—a policy of avenging defeat by ruining the prizes of the victors. What an utter contrast to the standards observed by his predecessors on the throne of Macedonia! These sovereigns had fought one another continuously in the open country but had rarely destroyed and wrecked the towns. This was a fact of general knowledge, established by the war which Alexander the Great waged against Darius for the empire of Asia and again by the struggle of Alexander's successors over his inheritance, when they fought Antigonus for the possession of Asia in coalition. Moreover, the policy of the successors in the second generation, down to Pyrrhus, had been the same. They were ready enough to stake their fortunes in battle in the open country and they left nothing undone in their efforts to overcome one another by force of arms, but they used to spare the towns in order that the victors might enjoy the dominion over them and might receive due honors at the hands of their subjects. On the other hand, to destroy the objects of contention in the war while leaving the war itself in existence was the act of a madman and of one far gone in the malady, yet that was precisely what Philip was doing now. In the course of his forced march from the pass in Epirus, Philip had wrecked in Thessaly more towns whose friend and ally he professed to be than had ever been wrecked by any power with whom the Thessalians were at war.

SEED ON GOOD GROUND
(SECOND CENTURY B.C.)
(POLYBIUS: Book VI, chapter 25, [3-11])

AT the present day, the equipment of the Roman cavalryman is practically identical with that of his Hellenic confrere. Originally, however, it was otherwise. In the first place, they used to wear no breastplates but went into action in their shirts—a kit which was convenient and practical enough for rapid mounting and dismounting, but which endangered their lives in hand-to-hand fighting owing to their going into action defenseless. Their lances, again, were unpractical in two ways. In the first place they made them so slender and fragile that they were unable to aim straight at their mark; while, before the lance head had time to strike a target, the lance itself was in most cases shivered to pieces by the vibration arising from the mere motion of the horse. In addition, they constructed their lances without spikes at the butt end and were therefore only able to deliver their one first thrust with the head, after which the weapon was broken and was of no practical use to them again. Furthermore, their shields were of oxhide and bore a strong resemblance to those wafers with a lump in the middle that are laid upon the bodies of sacrificial victims. These shields were impossible to employ for attacks because they possessed no rigidity, while the effect of rain upon them was to ruin the leather and to make them so sodden that they always were, and to this day still become, entirely unmanageable. In consequence, when experience proved their own equipment unsatisfactory, the Romans speedily replaced it by the Hellenic, which possesses the following advantages. To begin with, the first thrust of the lance, made with the head, is always well-aimed and effective, because the lance is constructed with a solid, rigid shaft, while at the same time the weapon can be made to last out during vigorous usage by reversing the spike end and the head end. The case is the same with the Hellenic type of shield, which possesses the rigidity and the handiness required for employment in attacks and charges. The Romans were not slow to borrow these advantages when once they had realized them, the fact being that they are without a rival among the nations of the world in their adaptability and their enthusiasm for progress.

SEED ON STONY GROUND
(SECOND CENTURY B.C.)
(POLYBIUS: Book XXXIX, chapter 1)

AULUS POSTUMIUS is worthy of remark from the following points of view. He came of a leading house and family, but was personally garrulous and loquacious and conceited to the last degree. From his early childhood he fell in love with the Hellenic language and system of education, and he threw himself into them in season and out of season to such excess that he succeeded in disgusting the older and most distinguished leaders of Roman society with the whole cult of Hellenism. He ended by actually attempting to write a poem and a transactional history, the preface of which he employed in beseeching his readers to forgive him if his Roman nationality prevented him from mastering the Hellenic language and the art of literary form. Thereby he exposed himself to a pertinent retort from Marcus Porcius Cato. "I am at a loss to imagine," said Cato, "on what ground he makes this appeal for mercy. Supposing that the Amphictyonic Council had given him orders to write a history, he might possibly have been justified in proffering these excuses by way of appeal; but to enroll himself, under no manner of compulsion, as a volunteer, and then to appeal for forgiveness if he writes bad Greek, is a symptom of thoroughgoing eccentricity. It is just as futile as if a man were to enter for a gymnastic competition like boxing or the pancratium [1] and then present himself in the ring at the time when the fight was due to begin, only in order to appeal to the spectators to forgive him if he failed to stand the exertion and the blows. A sportsman of this kidney would obviously deserve to be made a laughingstock and to receive his punishment out of hand; and the same thing ought to happen to the corresponding type of historian, to teach him to keep his presumptuous hands off a noble profession." Aulus Postumius maintained his consistency by enthusiastically cultivating in his private life the worst tendencies of Hellenic society. He was pleasure-loving and shy of hard work, and both vices are displayed in the facts of his career. Having been the first to arrive in Hellas at the time when the battle in Phocis [2] was fought, he pleaded indisposition as an excuse for retiring to Thebes, in order to avoid being involved in the danger; and then, when the battle was over, he was the first to write to the Senate announcing the victory, which he did with superfluous touches of vivid detail, as though he had participated personally in the action.

[1] A combination of boxing and wrestling. [ED.]
[2] Between the Romans and the Achaeans in 146 B.C. [ED.]

SEED AMONG THORNS
(*ca.* 175 B.C.)

(The Old Testament in Greek according to the Septuagint,
Cambridge, 1899, University Press, Vol. III: *Second
Book of Maccabees*: Chapter 4, verses 7–17)

AFTER the decease of Seleucus and the accession to the throne
of Antiochus the Illustrious (so-called), Jason, the brother of
Onias, wormed his way into the High Priesthood. He achieved
this by petitioning the King and promising him three hundred
and sixty talents of silver per annum, besides eighty talents
under other heads of revenue. In addition, he undertook to
levy a further hundred and fifty talents, if he were also em-
powered by royal authority to organize an athletic club and a
cadet corps,[1] and to register the inhabitants of Jerusalem as
citizens of Antioch. The King gave his consent; and so, as soon
as he had taken up the reins of office, the new High Priest set
about transforming his countrymen into Hellenes. He brushed
aside the royal benefactions secured to the Jews by the efforts
of John, the father of Eupolemos,[2] and he overthrew their
lawful institutions, which he replaced by illegal innovations.
He took peculiar pleasure in establishing an athletic club under the shadow of the citadel, enrolling the pick of our generation as members and putting them into sun hats. Thanks,
indeed, to the unparalleled profanity of Jason, who behaved
more like an enemy of religion than like a High Priest, Hellenism enjoyed such a vogue and Renegadism made such strides
that the priests lost interest in their ritual, looked down upon
the Temple, neglected the sacrifices, and cared for nothing
except to appear on the recreation ground and to take part in
the illegal performance called "Putting the Weight." They
despised what their forefathers had honored, and regarded
Hellenic ideas as the best in the world. In retribution for this,
they were overtaken by serious misfortunes and received their
punishment at the hands of the very nation whose ways they
had admired and wished to imitate in every particular, but
who turned out to be their worst enemies. The laws of Heaven
cannot be defied with impunity, as the sequel will show.

[1] In Greek: ἔφηβοι. [ED.]
[2] The John who went to Rome in order to negotiate a friendly alliance. [AUTHOR.]

DEPOPULATION
(SECOND CENTURY B.C.)

(POLYBIUS: Book XX, chapter 6, [1-6] and Book XXXVI, chapter 7)

THE public life of Boeotia had lapsed into such an unhealthy condition that the administration of justice in the country had remained in abeyance over a period of nearly twenty-five years. This had applied to private commercial suits as well as to cases involving a breach of the public peace. The operation of the judicature was perpetually frustrated on the part of the executive by proclamations of the state of siege or of federal mobilization. Some executive officers went so far as to distribute outdoor relief to the destitute out of public funds—a procedure which trained the masses to listen to the voice and secure the election of candidates whose return was calculated to save criminals and debtors from the arm of the law and to supplement private incomes in perpetuity out of the public purse owing to the complacency of the executive. The politician chiefly responsible for this unhealthy state of affairs was Opheltas, who was perpetually excogitating fresh measures which ostensibly benefited the majority of the population for the time being, although admittedly calculated in the long run to ruin the whole community.

The effect of these measures was reinforced by another obsession of an unfortunate kind. Persons dying childless began to abandon the habit which had formerly prevailed in Boeotia of bequeathing their property to their relatives in the next generation, and to spend it instead upon entertainment and drinking, in which they shared it with their friends. Even persons leaving families began, in many cases, to earmark the greater part of their property for legacies to the clubs, until there were many individuals in Boeotia entitled to more free dinners a month than there were days on which to eat them.

.   .   .   .   .   .

I now propose to discuss the issues raised by the question [of the part played by Fortune and Fate in public and private life], so far as is permissible within the limits of transactional history. Now there are certainly phenomena like continuous accesses of abnormal rain or snowfall, or, again, of abnormal droughts and frosts (with the consequent damage to crops in either case), or like continuous epidemics of disease, and so on, the causes of which it is difficult or impossible for the human mind to comprehend; and in such cases, where a cause is not easy to discover, there is some excuse for cutting the knot by attributing the phenomenon to God or to Fortune. In these situations, the lack of any rational alternative makes it not unreasonable to accept the guidance of popular beliefs and to attempt to propitiate Heaven by prayer and sacrifice, as we do when we send to inquire of the gods what we ought to say or do in order to alleviate our position and to secure a respite from the evils under which we are laboring. Where, however, it is possible to discover the cause which is the origin and object of the phenomenon, I feel that there is no justification for attributing it to the operations of Heaven. I am thinking of the following example. In our own times the whole of Hellas has been afflicted with a low birth rate or, in other words, with depopulation, through which the states have been emptied of inhabitants with an accompanying fall of productivity—and this in spite of the fact that we have not suffered from any continuous wars or epidemics. Now if, in this connection, anyone had suggested our sending to the Gods to inquire what we ought to say or do in order to increase our numbers and to reform our social life, he would undoubtedly have been regarded as no better than a fool—the cause being evident and the remedy in our own hands. The fact is that the people of Hellas had entered upon the false path of ostentation, avarice, and laziness, and were therefore becoming unwilling to marry or, if they did marry, to bring up the children born to them; the majority were only willing to bring up at most one or two, in order to leave them wealthy and to spoil them in their childhood; and in consequence of all this the evil had been spreading rapidly before it was observed. Where there are families of one or two children, of whom war claims one and disease the other for its victim, it is an evident and inevitable consequence that households should be left desolate and that states, precisely like beehives, should gradually lose their reserves and sink into impotence. On this subject there is no need whatsoever to inquire of the gods as to how we are to be saved from the cancer. The plain man will answer that, first and foremost, we must save ourselves, either by changing our obsession or alternatively by making it illegal not to bring up every child that is born.

THE CLASS WAR: SECOND PHASE
(*ca.* 140–131 B.C.)

(DIODORUS OF AGYRIUM: *Library of Universal History:* ed. by C. Müller, Paris, 1844, Didot, Vol. II; and by L. Dindorf, Leipzig, 1868, Teubner, Vol. V: Fragments of Books XXXIV-XXXV, Group 2)

(1) AFTER the overthrow of Carthage, Sicily had enjoyed sixty years of general prosperity, when she fell a victim to the Slave War. The origins of this catastrophe are to be sought in the great increase of affluence, leading to a corresponding accumulation of capital, which was invested in wholesale purchases of slaves. The unfortunate creatures were marched away in droves from the dealers' establishments, (27) until the whole of Sicily was deluged with such multitudes that the figures have been discredited as exaggerations. (2) Upon arrival, they were branded with the marks of their new owners, and the younger individuals were employed as cow boys, while the rest were assigned to various departments of labor. They were all shockingly overdriven, and practically no provision was made for feeding and clothing them. (27) The wealthier Sicilians vied with their Italian neighbors in arrogance, avarice and brutality, and the big Italian slaveowners actually trained their cow boys in criminal habits by refusing to serve out rations and then permitting them to live by brigandage. (28) This meant giving license to men with the physical strength to execute their will, the leisure and liberty to find their opportunity, and the pressure of hunger to force them into the most hazardous adventures; and inevitably there was a rapid increase in criminality. They began by murdering people traveling alone or two together on the open road. Then they started making night attacks upon the humbler farms in gangs, breaking in by force, plundering what they found, and killing anyone who resisted. (29) Their daring increased until it was impossible to travel in Sicily by night and dangerous to live out in the country in the old way. The island had become infested with brigandage, violence, and sudden death; and the cow boys, now equipped like soldiers and hardened to life in the open air, were naturally filled with more and more self-confidence and audacity. With bludgeons, spears, and massive shepherds' crooks in their hands, and wolf or boar skins protecting their bodies, they presented almost as formidable an appearance as if they had stepped off a battlefield. (30) The troops of powerful dogs at

their heels and the abundant meat and milk diet with which
their herds provided them, promoted their moral and physical
reversion toward savagery. It was as if the whole country were
infested with guerrillas. The slaves had been armed and em-
boldened by their masters' mismanagement; (3) and the governors, though they attempted preventive measures, were
afraid to inflict punishment on account of the power and influence of the magnates whose property the brigands were,
and were therefore compelled to give a free field to brigandage
in their province. The authorities, in fact, were thoroughly
intimidated by the men of property, who were mostly Roman
citizens belonging to the Order of Knighthood[1] and consequently serving on the juries which heard the prosecutions of
time-expired provincial officials.

(4) The hardship of the slaves' lives and the brutality and
wantonness of the physical injuries inflicted upon them at
length passed the bounds of endurance. They found opportunities to meet and plotted revolt, until they succeeded in trans-
lating their purpose into action. (5) One of the masters,
Antigenes of Enna, possessed a Syrian slave from Apaméa
with a turn for spiritualism and conjuring, who pretended to
foretell the future by dream messages and mystified numbers
of people by his natural aptitude in this direction. Gradually
he ventured further, until he not only told fortunes from
dreams but professed to see spirits, and to learn the future
from them, with his waking consciousness. (6) Some of his
many impostures happened by chance to come true, and those
which turned out otherwise were not detected, while those
which succeeded attracted attention, so that his reputation
grew. Eventually he discovered a trick for working himself
into a state of exaltation and emitting fire and flame from his
mouth, as a *mise en scène* for declaiming his prophecies.[2]
(7) Before the revolt, this impostor had already begun to say
that the Syrian Goddess had appeared to him in a vision and
had hailed him as king, and he actually reiterated this to his
own master as well as to others. (8) Most people treated the
affair as a joke, but Antigenes was fascinated by the conjuring,
and promoted Eunus (as the conjurer was called) to appear
at his dinner parties, where he used to cross-examine him regarding his kingdom and how he would behave, when king,
toward the various guests of the evening. Eunus used to tell
his story without turning a hair, explain how kind he would

---

[1] Roman knights in the second century B.C. were drawn from much the same
social class as British knights in the twentieth century A.D. [ED.]
[2] Apparently he inserted burning matter, with enough fuel to keep it alight,
into a nutshell or something of the kind with a hole at either end; held this in
his mouth; and breathed out either sparks or flame at will by blowing into it.
[AUTHOR.]

be to the masters, and perform so extravagantly that the whole company would shake with laughter. Guests used to take handsome helpings from the table and present them to him, with the request that when he entered his kingdom he would remember the favor. (9) As it turned out, the foolery ended in his becoming king in truth and deed, and those who had shown him mock deference at dinner were recompensed for their favors in sober earnest.[1]

(10) The actual outbreak of the revolt was due to Damophilus of Enna, a particularly arrogant multimillionaire. (34) He farmed a vast number of acres, owned immense herds of stock, and tried to outbid the Italian settlers in the island not only in luxury but in the quantity of his slaves and the inhuman harshness with which he treated them. He traveled round his estates in a four-wheeled carriage with thoroughbred horses and a retinue of armed slaves. He also made a point of having round him a troupe of pretty boys and a bevy of ill-bred hangers-on. (35) In his town and country residences he made an elaborate display of plate and purple, and gave banquets of a royal arrogance and of a profusion which put the proverbial luxury of Persia into the shade. Indeed, he was more than Persian not only in his extravagance but in his arrogance. It was the old story of an ill-bred and uncultivated character finding itself in possession of irresponsible power and unearned riches, and the chain of excess and pride duly terminated in the destruction of Damophilus himself and in a great disaster for his country.

(38) On one occasion, when some of his slaves presented themselves naked and broached the question of new clothes, Damophilus refused to listen to them; asked them angrily whether the travelers on the public highway went naked and were not an obvious source of supply for anyone in want of an outfit; ordered them to be bound to the pillars of his porch, and sent them away with a whipping like the arrogant brute that he was. (37) Not a day passed without this headstrong and savage monster inflicting quite unjustifiable injuries upon one or other of his slaves; and his wife Megallis, who took as much pleasure as he did in administering punishment, was guilty of equally arrogant and savage behavior to her maids and to the other slaves under her orders. (10) Their victims became so infuriated that they agreed to rebel and to murder

---

[1] (41) After his proclamation as king, Eunus put all [the slaveowners] to death with the sole exception of those persons who, under the old regime, had welcomed him at dinner parties or at his spiritualist séances when he went out into society with his master, and who had shown their good will by presenting him with portions from the table. These persons he now surreptitiously set at liberty—an extraordinary instance, this, of the reversal of Fortune that benefits conferred upon the meanest of God's creatures should be recompensed in due course by such an overwhelming token of gratitude. [AUTHOR.]

their master and mistress; (24*b*) and, having made up their minds, they addressed themselves to Eunus (who resided in the neighborhood) in order to ascertain if success would be granted to their endeavors by the Powers Unseen.

Eunus worked himself up, went through his usual performances, heard what they had come to ask, and vouchsafed that the Powers would crown their revolt with success on condition that they made no delay in putting their plans into execution. Fate, he added, had designated as theirs his own town of Enna, the center and citadel of the island. This language, which they interpreted to mean that Heaven would be with them in their enterprise, so completely won them over to the idea of revolt that they did not delay a moment longer. They immediately liberated their companions in chains, mustered the hands from neighboring estates, and collected a band of four hundred at a plantation close to Enna. An agreement was made; an oath of mutual loyalty was taken over a nocturnal sacrifice; and the conspirators armed themselves as best they could. The most formidable weapon that came to their hands was their thirst for the blood of their arrogant masters. Eunus took command, and, raising a war cry, they surprised the town about midnight, (12) broke into the houses, and started a general massacre, not even sparing babes at the breast, but tearing them from their mothers' arms and dashing them against the stones. Their outrages upon the women, committed before their husbands' eyes, are too obscene to be described. They were reinforced by numbers of town slaves, who proceeded to extremities against their respective masters before they took their part in the indiscriminate massacre.

(13) Eunus and his band discovered that Damophilus was staying with his wife in their suburban villa. A detachment was dispatched to arrest them, and they were dragged from their retreat with their hands bound behind their backs, undergoing every kind of maltreatment on the way. (39) They had, however, a young unmarried daughter of a particularly unspoiled and humane disposition, who invariably did her utmost to intercede for slaves sentenced by her parents to floggings and to relieve those in chains. Her goodness had won her intense and universal affection, and on this terrible occasion the gratitude which she had earned enlisted on her behalf the better feelings of her former protégés. No one ventured to lay a violent hand upon her, and her honor was scrupulously respected by all concerned. The most efficient members of the band (the keenest being a certain Hermēas) were detailed to escort her to some relations at Catana. (13) This was a demonstration that the treatment meted out

to the others was not the expression of any innate barbarity in the slaves, but was simply retribution for the wrongs which had previously been inflicted upon them.

(14) Meanwhile, Damophilus and Megallis, after being dragged into town by the detachment, were marched into the theater, where the mass of the insurgents was by this time assembled. Damophilus attempted to engineer his salvation and was making appeals to many individuals in the crowd, when Hermeas and Zeuxis, who were embittered against him, denounced him as a fraud and butchered him—one with a sword thrust through the ribs and the other with a blow on the neck from an ax—without waiting for a regular trial by the assembly. This was followed by the election of Eunus as king, not for courage or military ability but merely for his conjuring powers and because he had started the revolt. They also hoped that his name might influence the superstitious feelings of his new subjects in favor[1] of the cause.

(15) Having thus become absolute master of the rebels, Eunus proceeded to call a public meeting; put to death such citizens of Enna as had received quarter, with the exception of the armorers, who were set to work in chains; and handed Megallis over to the mercy of her maids. After torturing her, they threw her over a precipice, while Eunus likewise put to death his own masters, Antigenes and Python. (16) The new sovereign assumed the diadem and other insignia of royalty; proclaimed his consort queen;[2] appointed the best brains as councilors, among them Achaeus;[3] equipped more than six thousand men as best he could within three days; formed a reserve armed with axes, hatchets, slings, scythes, fire-hardened stakes and kitchen spits, and began to overrun the whole country, pillaging as he went. Immense numbers of slaves flocked to him, until he ventured to measure swords with Roman troops and won several engagements by weight of numbers, having by that time at his disposal more than ten thousand men.

(17) At this point another slave revolt was started by a Cilician named Cleon—a development which excited a widespread hope that the two parties of insurgents would come into conflict and would rid Sicily of the class war by exterminating one another. Contrary to expectation, however, they made common cause. Cleon submitted quietly to Eunus at

---

[1] The Greek word Εὔνοια, "favor," is derived from Εὔνους, "favorable." [ED.]

[2] She was a Syrian from the same town as himself. [AUTHOR.]

[3] Achaeus, who came from the country whose name he bore, distinguished himself equally in counsel and in action. (42) Disapproving of the proceedings of the runaways, he had repeatedly censured their excesses and quite openly prophesied that they would meet with prompt retribution. Notwithstanding this frankness, Eunus never dreamed of putting him to death, and not only presented him with the mansion of his former owners but made him a Councilor of State. [AUTHOR.]

the mere word of command and accepted the rank of general under his royal authority, with a force under his own orders of five thousand men. This happened about a month after the beginning of the rebellion. (18) Shortly afterward, Lucius Hypsaeus arrived from Rome to take over the command of eight thousand troops raised in Sicily, whereupon the insurgents took up the gauntlet and were victorious. At that moment they were twenty thousand strong, but before long two hundred thousand had gathered to their standards, and they conducted a succession of campaigns against the Romans in which they acquitted themselves with credit and established a superiority. (19) As the news spread, slave revolts flared up everywhere. At Rome a hundred and fifty individuals entered into a conspiracy, in Attica over a thousand, and others in Delos and elsewhere. These movements were quickly suppressed by the prompt action and appalling severity of the responsible authorities on the spot, who thus succeeded in checking unrest in other areas where it was on the point of outbreak; (20) but in Sicily the situation went from bad to worse. Towns were captured with their entire populations and one army after another was cut to pieces by the insurgents, until the Roman commander Rupilius recovered Tauromenium for his government. The siege was vigorously conducted and the rebels were reduced to such extremities of hunger that they took to cannibalism.[1] Cleon's brother Comanus was captured in an attempt to escape from the besieged city, (21) and at last the citadel was treacherously surrendered by a Syrian named Sarapion. All the runaways in the town fell into the commander's hands and were thrown over a precipice, after torture. Rupilius advanced to Enna, started to besiege it as he had done with Tauromenium, and reduced the rebels to the verge of despair. General Cleon made a sortie with a few comrades and met a heroic death in action. The display of his corpse, covered with wounds, led in turn to the treacherous surrender of Enna, which was so strong a natural fortress that it could never have been taken by storm. (22) Eunus, with his bodyguard of a thousand men, fled, like a coward, to a position protected by precipices. His followers realized that there was no escape for them (the Roman commander was already moving against them in person) and proceeded to decapitate one another with their swords. The conjurer-king lost his morale, skulked in a ravine, and was dragged out with four attendants—his cook, his baker, his masseur, and his entertainer. (23) He was consigned to prison at Morgantinē, where he died of worms—an end well merited by his

---

[1] They began by eating the children and went through the women, while there were isolated cases of men devouring one another. [AUTHOR.]

criminal career. Rupilius scoured the whole island with a flying column of picked troops and cleared it of brigandage more rapidly than anyone had thought possible.

(48) When Sicily was overtaken by these overwhelming disasters, the freeborn proletariat, so far from sympathizing with the victims, actually exulted over them out of resentment at the existing inequalities of wealth and condition. This long-standing resentment was transformed from a painful into a gratifying emotion at the spectacle of magnificence reduced to the level of the misery upon which it had previously looked down with disdain. The most serious feature was that the insurgents, who took long and rational views, refrained from burning the farms or injuring the property and the stocks of agricultural produce which they found in them, and did not molest persons devoting their energies to work on the land; whereas the social resentment of the free proletariat was so profound that they offered their services against the slaves simply as a pretext for going out into the country and not only pillaging property but burning farms.

DEBASEMENT
(53 B.C.)

(PLUTARCH: *Parallel Lives*: Teubner text, ed. by C. Sintenis, Vol. III: *Marcus Crassus,* chapters 32–33)

SURĒNAS[1] dispatched Crassus's head and hand to King Hyrōdes [2] in Armenia, but sent messages on his own account to Seleucia [3] in order to spread the report that he was bringing back Crassus alive—after which, he proceeded to organize a burlesque procession and to insult Rome by entitling it a *triumph.* Gaius Paccianus, the prisoner who bore the closest personal resemblance to Crassus, was dressed up in the robes of a queen; instructed to answer to the names of "Crassus" and "General" when addressed by them; and then led along on horseback, with trumpeters and lictors [4] mounted on camels riding before him. Purses were suspended from the lictors' rods, while the axes were decorated with the severed heads of fresh-killed Roman soldiers. The procession was

[1] The title of the Parthian commander who had just destroyed a Roman army commanded by Crassus at Carrhae in Northwest Mesopotamia. [ED.]
[2] The King of Parthia, who had been operating against the Armenian allies of Rome. [ED.]
[3] A Hellenic colony founded by Seleucus, one of Alexander the Great's successors, in 'Iraq, at a point on the Tigris opposite Ctesiphon and below the later site of Baghdad. [ED.]
[4] The official attendants attached to senior executive officers of the Roman Government. [ED.]

closed by Seleucian prostitutes playing music and singing topical songs of a scurrilous and burlesque character, in which Crassus was satirized for his effeminacy and unmanliness. This show was open to the public, but Surenas also convened the municipal council of Seleucia and laid before them a parcel of obscene literature, consisting of the *Milesian Tales* of Aristides, which unhappily were genuine enough. They had been discovered among Roscius's baggage and they presented Surenas with a text for a serio-comic tirade against the Romans, who "even on active service are unable to keep away from subjects and publications of this character." The result, however, was only to confirm the Seleucians' belief in the wisdom of Aesop, when they saw Surenas with his bag full of Milesian obscenities duly buckled on in front of him, while behind he was trailing all the time a Parthian Sybaris[1] in the shape of carriage after carriage full of concubines. Indeed, his parade was in many respects a replica of such reptiles as the *Echidna* and the *Stick Snake,* presenting as it did its prominent foreparts bristling with a terrifying and ferocious array of spears and small arms and chargers, whereas the rear of the column tailed off into ballets and cymbals and chorus music and obscene night life with improper women. If Roscius was open to censure, the Parthians on their side were shameless in passing it upon his *Milesian Tales,* considering how many sovereigns who had sat on the throne of Arsaces had been the issue of Milesian and Ionian mistresses.

In the meantime Hyrodes had successfully effected a reconciliation with Artawasdes of Armenia and had arranged the betrothal of Artawasdes's daughter to his own son Pacŏrus. They were now engaged in giving mutual banquets and drinking parties, which were enlivened by the presentation of a number of Hellenic variety turns. Hyrodes was by no means unfamiliar with the language and literature of Hellas, while Artawasdes was actually the author of tragedies, speeches, and histories, some of which have been preserved. At the moment when Crassus's head arrived at the palace, the dining tables had just been removed and an actor of tragedy named Jason of Trallēs was singing Agāvē's part in the *Bacchae* of Euripides. He was already scoring a success when Sillaces presented himself at the door of the audience chamber, did his obeisance, and flung the head of Crassus into the midst of the company. The Parthians seized up the object amid clapping of hands and shouts of exultation; Sillaces was given a seat by the chamberlains at the King's express desire;

[1] A Hellenic colony in the Toe of Italy which had become a byword for self-indulgence in the sixth century B.C. [ED.]

and then Jason, after handing the dummy head of Pentheus
to a member of the chorus, picked up the head of Crassus,
threw himself into the Bacchic ecstasy, and proceeded to chant,
in an exalted strain, the lines which run:

> Lo, from the trunk new-shorn
> Hither a mountain thorn
> Bear we! O Asia-born
> Bacchanals, bless this chase![1]

This enchanted the whole company, but when the performance reached the dialogue between Agave and the chorus:

> *Chorus:* Who first came nigh him?
> *Agave:* I, I, 'tis confessed![1]

Pomaxathres, who happened to be one of the guests, sprang
to his feet and tried to snatch away the head, on the ground
that he had a better right to recite these words than the performer. The King, who was delighted, presented Pomaxathres
with the traditional Parthian decorations and gave Jason a
talent, and this is supposed to have been the last act of that
tragedy in real life which was Crassus's Asiatic command.

There is some satisfaction in recording that the savagery
of Hyrodes and the perjury of Surenas met with the retribution which they deserved. Surenas was put to death not long
afterward by Hyrodes, who was jealous of his glory, while
Hyrodes himself lived to lose his son Pacorus in a disastrous
battle with the Romans and then sickened with a malady
which determined in dropsy. At this juncture, poison was
treacherously administered to him by his son Phraates, and
when this poison was absorbed by the malady and was excret-
ed with it, to the relief of the organism, Phraates took the
shortest cut and strangled him.

ATHENS

(*ca.* A.D. 52–53)

(*The Acts of the Apostles:* Chapter XVII, verses 16–34)

WHILE Paul was waiting at Athens for his companions, his
inmost spirit was revolted at the spectacle of a city so terribly
infested with images. He was giving addresses in the syna-
gogue to the Jews and their converts, and every day in the
piazza to all who stopped to listen, and here he had encoun-

---

[1] Quoted from Gilbert Murray's translation. [ED.]

ters with some of the Stoic and Epicurean philosophers. Some said: "What does this scrap-gatherer mean?" Others: "He appears to be a proclaimer of foreign divinities"—because Paul was preaching Jesus and Resurrection.[1] So they took him with them to the Areopagus,[2] saying: "Can you explain exactly what this strange teaching of yours is? There is something foreign to our ideas in the doctrines which we are hearing for the first time from you. We should like to learn what they mean." [3] So Paul took his stand in the middle of the Areopagus and spoke as follows:

"Gentlemen, I see at every turn in Athens how a sense of religion obsesses you. I was exploring and examining the objects of your worship when I came upon an altar inscribed: 'To an Unknown God.' It is this, which you are worshiping in ignorance, that I am declaring to you. The God who has created the Universe and all that is in it, being Lord of Heaven and Earth, does not live in hand-built temples or receive services at the hands of men to satisfy any needs, for He Himself gives to all creatures life and breath and everything; and He has made, from one ancestor, every nation of men to live on the whole face of the Earth and has appointed beforehand periods for their existence and boundaries for their habitation, that they might look for God and perhaps feel their way toward Him and find Him—though in fact He is not far from any one of us, for in Him we live and move and are, as some of your own poets[4] also have said:

And we are his children.

But if we are the children of God, we ought not to imagine that the Deity is like gold or silver or marble—a thing carved by human art and imagination.

"Now the Times of Ignorance[5] have been passed over by God, but today He is proclaiming to Mankind that all men everywhere must repent, since He has set a day on which He is going to 'judge the world in righteousness,' in the person of a man appointed by Him; and He has given a proof of this for all men by raising that man from the dead."

But when he spoke of dead men being raised, some of them began to jeer, while others said: "We will listen to you again on this subject another time." So Paul went out from the

[1] In Greek 'Ανάστασις, a feminine noun which might be the name of a goddess. [ED.]

[2] An outlying spur of the Acropolis, on which the earliest town council of Athens had originally held its sessions. [ED.]

[3] The citizens of Athens as well as the alien residents in the country appeared to devote their whole time to propounding or receiving new ideas. [AUTHOR.]

[4] *E.g.* Cleanthes the Stoic (300-220 B.C.) and Arātus of Soli (*ca.* 270 B.C.), the poet of Astronomy. [ED.]

[5] A conception that reappears in Islam. [ED.]

meeting, but certain individuals attached themselves to him and believed, including Dionysius (a member of the Areopagus Council), a woman named Damaris, and others besides.

CIMMERIAN DARKNESS
(*ca.* A.D. 54–68)

(EUNAPIUS OF SARDIS: Fragment 54=*Historici Graeci Minores:* Teubner text, Vol. I, pp. 246–248)

THE following incident is reported to have occurred in the reign of Nero, though in this case only a single community was affected. The story is that an actor of tragedy, driven from Rome by Nero's professional jealousy, took occasion to go on tour with the idea of displaying his vocal accomplishments to a semi-civilized public. His travels brought him to the great and populous town of [Seville],[1] where he collected an audience in the theater. On the first day, when the audience had taken their seats, his performance miscarried. The spectators could not face the spectacle with which they had just been presented for the first time in their lives, and crushed and trampled one another in a wild flight from the auditorium. The actor then interviewed the notables of the town in private, explained the mechanism of the mask and of the stands which exaggerate the relative height of the performer, and by this method gradually induced them to nerve themselves for bearing the spectacle. After these preliminaries he appeared again before an audience which was still only just in a condition to support the sight of him. This time he began by giving them a mild and gentle taste of his voice and melody;[2] but, as he progressed, he produced his voice in fuller volume, then relaxed it, then introduced an austere note, and followed this by reversion to a honeyed tone. The season happened to be summer, which was at its sultriest in the theater, and the actor therefore urged his audience to repose themselves and to attend his performance in the cool of the evening. At this, the audience fell at his feet and besought him, as they groveled there, in every accent of appeal never to deprive them of the blissful pleasure which they were now enjoying. Thereupon the actor let himself go and threw himself into his part. It is true that, in the process of transmission to so unintelligent an audience, most of the graces of Tragedy had fallen away—for instance, the majesty and

[1] The name in the text of the MS. is uncertain. [ED.]
[2] The piece which he was acting was the *Andromeda* of Euripides. [AUTHOR.]

impressiveness of the phraseology with all its possibilities, the charm of the rhythm, the interpretation of character with its exquisitely fine capacity for reaching the emotions through the ear, and (last but not least) a familiarity with the plot. Yet, in spite of being stripped of all these auxiliaries, the performer so enthralled his audience by the mere beauty of his elocution and his singing that they did obeisance to him as if he were a God when they left the theater and brought him their choicest possessions as gifts, until the recipient found himself embarrassed at his riches. A week after the performance, however, an epidemic suddenly descended upon the town, and there lay the whole population in the streets, extenuated by the attacks of a virulent diarrhea, yet never ceasing to declaim—not the words of the play with any articulateness but the tune, to the best of each sufferer's natural ability. The hand of *Andromeda* was indeed heavy upon them, and the town was so seriously depleted of its population, male and female, that it had to be repeopled from the environs.

THE CONFLICT OF CIVILIZATIONS
(A.D. 66)

(JOSEPHUS OF JERUSALEM: *History of the Romano-Jewish War*: Book II, sections 449–498)

THE population [of Jerusalem] still hoped to find some means of repairing the breach of the peace completely;[1] but the motive of Eleazer's party in killing Menahem[2] had been not to put an end to the war but to secure a freer hand for waging it. In any case, the earnest entreaties to relinquish the siege,[3] which the population addressed to the militants, only caused the latter to redouble the fierceness of their assaults. At length the resisting power of Metilius's[4] men gave out and they made overtures to Eleazer's forces. They asked for a bare guarantee of their lives, while offering to surrender their arms

---

[1] Peace between the Jewish population of the province of Judaea and the Roman Government had already been broken by armed and organized Jewish fanatics, who had delivered attacks and inflicted casualties upon some of the detachments of Roman troops in occupation of various strategic points in Jerusalem; but the main struggle hitherto had been among the Jews themselves, between the moderates who wanted to avoid a breach with Rome and the extremists who wanted to insure one. [ED.]

[2] Eleazer appears to have been a disinterested and Menahem a self-seeking fanatic. [ED.]

[3] The Romanophil Jews had already capitulated to the fanatics on condition of abandoning their Roman comrades in arms, and, after this, the survivors of the various Roman detachments had concentrated in the three forts of Hippicus, Phasael, and Mariammē. [ED.]

[4] Metilius was the Roman commander. [AUTHOR.]

and other property. The besiegers caught at their appeal for mercy and sent up to them Gorio, son of Nicomēdes, Ananias, son of Sadducī, and Judas, son of Jonathan, to ratify the agreement. This done, Metilius proceeded to evacuate his men. So long as they were still under arms, none of the insurgents either made any attempt upon them or betrayed any sinister intentions; but as soon as they had all laid down their shields and swords, in accordance with the terms agreed upon, and were retreating without further suspicion, Eleazer's men threw themselves upon them, surrounded them, and started a massacre. The Romans neither attempted to defend themselves nor asked for quarter, but simply invoked aloud the agreement and the oath of ratification. In this brutal fashion they were slaughtered to the last man.[1]

For Rome, this disaster was almost insensible. Her inexhaustible man power had merely been diminished by a few lives. To the Jews, on the contrary, it seemed like a prelude to their own annihilation. They realized that the breach of the peace was now irreparable, and they saw their country soiled with so deadly a stain of guilt that the wrath of Heaven might well be expected to descend upon her, quite apart from the vengeance of Rome. Consequently, there was general lamentation; disheartenment reigned throughout Jerusalem; and every moderate-minded citizen was filled with dismay at the thought that he would have to pay for the insurgents' crimes in his own person. What made it worse, the massacre had occurred on a Sabbath—a day on which the Jewish religion requires the suspension even of legitimate activities.

At the same hour of the same day, as though by supernatural prevision, the people of Caesarēa[2] were massacring the Jewish colony in their town—to such effect that over 20,000 had been slaughtered within a single hour and Caesarea left without a single Jewish inhabitant.[3] At the news of the blow at Caesarea, the whole Jewish nation ran amok. Dividing their forces, they started to devastate the villages inhabited by Syrians[4] as well as the neighboring towns—Philadelphia, Sebonītis, Gerasa, Pella, Scythopolis. Next, they fell upon Gadara, Hippus, and the Gaulanītis, stormed some places and set fire to others, and marched on against Cedasa,[5]

[1] With the sole exception of Metilius, who did ask for quarter and promised to go to the length of circumcision in turning Jew, in consideration of which they spared his life. [AUTHOR.]

[2] One of the principal towns in the coastal plain of Palestine. The majority of the inhabitants consisted of partially Hellenized Philistines living under the institutions of an autonomous Hellenic city-state. [ED.]

[3] Even the refugees were arrested by [the Roman governor] Florus and taken to be imprisoned in the dockyard. [AUTHOR.]

[4] I.e., populations that spoke Aramaic, like the Jews, but did not share the Jews' religion and were therefore in sympathy with Hellenic civilization and with the Roman Government. [ED.]

[5] The dependency of Tyre. [AUTHOR.]

Ptolemais, Gaba, Caesarea. Even Sebastē[1] and Ascalon failed to resist their impetus, and they followed up the burning of these places by razing Anthēdon and Gaza to the ground. In the circuit of each of these towns, great numbers of villages were wrecked, and there was no limit to the number of the male prisoners slaughtered.

At the same time the Syrians were massacring the Jews upon at least as large a scale. On their side, too, they began to butcher any Jews caught in their towns—not only out of hatred, as on former occasions, but with the additional motive, now, of forestalling the danger to which they were themselves exposed. Terrible disorder prevailed throughout the whole of Syria; every town was divided into two armed camps; and the safety of one party depended upon forestalling the other. The population passed their days in bloodshed, while their nights were rendered still more intolerable by terror. Even when they felt that they had disposed of the actual Jews, each community remained suspicious of the converts to Judaism, and while nobody, in any given community, could bring himself readily to massacre the doubtful class, the latter nevertheless remained an object of fear as an obstinately alien element in their midst. Even people with an established reputation for extreme humanity were excited by avarice into butchering their enemies. The murderers plundered the property of their victims without fear of punishment and transferred the spoils of the dead to their own houses as freely as if they had taken them on the field of battle. The palm was to those who could show the greatest gains, as an earnest of triumph over the greatest number of enemies. The eye was greeted by the spectacle of towns choked with unburied bodies, of infants and graybeards cast out lifeless side by side, of women not even shrouded to the minimum required by decency, and of the entire province pervaded by indescribable calamities— though the outrages actually perpetrated at any given moment were dwarfed by the tense expectation of the further outrages threatened.

Up to this point the Jews had come into collision with non-Jews only, but in their incursion against Scythopolis they encountered the hostility of the local Jewish population. The local Jews here ranged themselves with the citizens and so far preferred their own security to the claims of kinship as to measure swords with their compatriots. Their very excess of zeal involved them, however, in suspicion. At any rate, the people of Scythopolis became afraid that their Jewish neighbors might make an attempt upon the town by night and might purchase forgiveness from their kinsmen for the deser-

[1] *I.e.,* Samaria. [ED.]

tion of their cause at the price of inflicting a terrible calamity upon the remainder of the population. They therefore called upon the Jewish colony, if they wished to confirm the good understanding between them and to prove their good faith toward their non-Jewish fellow townsmen, to remove with their families to the Grove.[1] The Jews obeyed orders without suspicion, whereafter the citizens kept quiet for two days in order to lull them into security; but on the third night they watched for a moment when some were off their guard and others asleep in order to slaughter them all.[2]

A memorable incident in these atrocities was the tragedy of Simon, the son of a prominent Jew named Saul. Simon was a man of exceptional physical strength and courage, and he had abused both qualities to the bane of his compatriots. Day by day he had gone into action, inflicted heavy casualties upon the Jews operating against Scythopolis, and frequently routed their total forces single-handed. In fact, he had turned the balance in the struggle. This renegade was entrapped by the punishment which he deserved for shedding the blood of his brethren. At the moment when the citizens of Scythopolis, after surrounding their Jewish fellow townsmen, were striking them down from one end to another of the Grove, Simon drew his sword; but, instead of turning upon any of the enemy (whose numbers he saw to be inexhaustible), he cried aloud in passionate remorse: "Citizens, my fate is worthy of my conduct toward you. In order to guarantee my good will in your regard, I have slaughtered multitudes of my own kinsfolk, and now my alien allies have proved as treacherous as was only to be expected, while my kinsfolk have suffered the last extremity of outrage at my hands. Therefore, by these same hands, I elect to die the death of the damned, which it was not for the enemy to inflict upon me. This fate will be at once a worthy punishment for my abominable crime and a testimony to my valor. I will have no enemy boast himself my slayer or falsely triumph over my corpse." With these words he cast a glance, in which pity and fury were mingled, upon his family around him—wife and children and aged father and mother. First he seized his father by his gray hairs and ran him through with his sword. Next, he found a willing victim in his mother, and then in his wife and children in succession. Each member of the household almost pressed forward to meet the blade in their eagerness to forestall the enemy. When he had dispatched his whole family, Simon mounted upon the corpses where every eye

[1] Some grove dedicated to one of the tutelary deities of Scythopolis and presumably situated outside the *enceinte* of the town. [ED.]
[2] The number of victims was over 13,000, and in every case their property was plundered by the murderers. [AUTHOR.]

could see him, extended his right arm with a gesture that none could mistake, and then plunged the sword into his own throat up to the hilt. While he deserved compassion for the prowess of his magnificent young body and for the fortitude of his soul, his tragic end was the logical penalty for giving his loyalty to alien allies.

The massacre at Scythopolis precipitated other murderous outbreaks against the respective Jewish colonies in the remaining towns. Two thousand five hundred Jews were slaughtered at Ascalon and two thousand at Ptolemais, where great numbers were also placed in rigorous confinement. At Tyre, they took many Jewish lives, but interned the majority of the Jewish population. At Hippus and Gadara, likewise, they disposed of the bolder spirits but kept the cowed majority under guard. The remaining cities of Syria followed the promptings of their respective hatred or fear of the Jewish elements among them. Only Antioch, Sidon, and Apamēa showed mercy to their Jewish residents and refused to allow any Jew to be put to death or imprisoned. Possibly the consciousness of their own superiority in numbers may have inspired them with a contempt for their Jewish neighbors' capacity to create disturbances, but in my belief their dominant motive was one of compassion toward neighbors whom they saw to be innocent of revolutionary intentions. At Gerasa they not only inflicted no injury upon the Jews who stayed behind, but escorted to the frontier those who elected to migrate from the municipal territory.

King Agrippa's dominions[1] were likewise the scene of a conspiracy against the Jews. The King himself had already gone to join Cestius Gallus[2] at Antioch, leaving the administration in the hands of one of his courtiers called Noar, a blood relation of King Dhu Aym,[3] when there arrived from Batanaea[4] a deputation of seventy [Jewish] notables, representing the best families and the best intelligence in the district, to ask for troops, in order to provide them with a garrison strong enough to suppress insurrection in case the disturbances spread to their area. This whole deputation was massacred by Noar, who detailed a detachment of the royal bodyguard

---

[1] Herod Agrippa was the great-grandson of Herod the Great and the son of another Herod Agrippa, under whose scepter the Romans had reunited Herod the Great's dominions. In A.D. 44, when the elder Agrippa died, the Roman Government took over the administration of Judaea as an agency of the Roman province of Syria, and confined the young Agrippa's dominions to a group of districts, east and northeast of the Sea of Galilee, which are now included not in Palestine but in the French mandated territory of Syria. The encounter between the younger Agrippa and Paul (*Acts of the Apostles*, chapters xxv–xxvi) must have occurred half a dozen years before the outbreak of the Romano-Jewish War. [ED.]

[2] The Roman governor of Syria. [ED.]

[3] Dhu Aym (Soaemus) of Homs (Emesa), who had been promoted by Nero's Government to be King of Diyar Bakr (Sophēnē). [ED.]

[4] Bashan, one of the districts in Agrippa's kingdom. [ED.]

to attack them by night. He ventured upon the crime without the concurrence of Agrippa. His motive was an avarice so insatiable that it led him into committing a deliberate outrage upon his compatriots at the cost of bringing the kingdom to destruction. He continued thereafter to indulge in savage excesses against the Jewish nation, until at length it came to the ears of Agrippa, whereupon the King dismissed him from his intendancy and was only restrained from putting him to death by consideration for King Dhu Aym.

On the other side, the Jewish insurgents captured a fort called Cyprus, commanding Jericho, where they massacred the garrison and razed the fortifications to the ground. At approximately the same date, the Jewish community at Machaerus started negotiations with the Roman garrison for the evacuation of the position and its surrender to them. In their anxiety to save the fortress from being taken by storm, the Romans capitulated on condition of marching out under safe-conduct, and they duly surrendered the fortress after receiving their guarantees. The Jews of Machaerus thereupon garrisoned the place in force themselves.

At Alexandria, the Jewish element had suffered from the perpetual hostility of the natives since the time when Alexander had permitted the Jews[1] to reside in the city upon an equal footing with the Hellenes. This privilege was confirmed to the Jews of Alexandria by Alexander's successors, who further assigned to them a special quarter of their own, in order to facilitate the maintenance of their ritual purity in daily life by diminishing their occasions of contact with non-Jews. At the same time, these sovereigns granted them the status of Macedonians.[2] When the Romans obtained possession of Egypt, neither the first Caesar nor any emperor who followed him was prepared to diminish the privileges which the Jews had enjoyed since the epoch of Alexander. There were ceaseless collisions, however, between the Jews and the Hellenes, and the penalties inflicted almost daily by the Roman governors upon numerous members of either community only served to exasperate the feud. On the present occasion, when disorders had broken out elsewhere, passions at Alexandria became more inflamed than ever. The Hellenic citizens were holding an assembly to discuss a deputation which they were proposing to send to Nero, when crowds of Jews flocked into the amphitheater together with the Hellenes. Their opponents had

---

[1] As a reward for the enthusiastic support which he had received from them against the Egyptians. [AUTHOR.]

[2] Both Alexander the Great and his general Ptolemy, son of Lāgus, who was his successor in Egypt and who founded the dynasty which ruled it until its annexation by Rome, were Hellenes of Macedonian nationality, and the Macedonian colony in Egypt therefore ranked above the Hellenic residents of other origin. [ED.]

no sooner espied them than they began to raise an uproar against them as enemies and spies, which ended in their springing to their feet and assaulting them. All but three of the Jews in the amphitheater dispersed in flight, but the three who were caught were dragged off to be burnt alive. Thereat, the whole Jewish colony started up to the rescue. They began by pelting the Hellenes with stones; then they snatched up torches and rushed for the amphitheater, threatening to make a holocaust of the Hellenic citizen body. What is more, they would have succeeded in doing so, had not their fury been forcibly repressed by Tiberius Alexander,[1] the governor of the city. In bringing them to their senses, Tiberius did not resort in the first instance to military measures. He began by sending his friends to them unobtrusively with entreaties not to provoke the intervention of the Roman forces. The insurgents, however, merely poured contempt upon these entreaties and vituperation upon Tiberius himself, until the governor realized that nothing short of a great catastrophe would check their revolutionary frenzy. Accordingly, he launched against them the two Roman legions which constituted the garrison of the city, reinforced by five thousand troops which had arrived by chance from North-West Africa to the Jews' undoing. He licensed these forces not only to take life but to plunder the property and burn down the houses of their victims; so the troops threw themselves upon the "Delta"[2] and began to carry out their orders, though not without some cost to themselves. The Jews collected their forces, placed their best-equipped fighting men in the front line, and resisted to the last possible moment. When once they broke, however, there were no limits to the carnage and their fate was annihilation. Some were caught in the open, others were herded into the houses, which the Romans proceeded to set on fire after first looting their contents. The troops were affected neither by pity for infancy nor by reverence for old age, but performed their butchers' work without respect of persons, until the whole quarter was swimming with blood and the death roll stood at the figure of fifty thousand. Even the remnant would not have been spared if they had not begged for quarter. Their supplication moved Alexander to take pity on them and he ordered the troops to retire. The troops themselves stopped the slaughter at a nod, with the obedience that comes of discipline; but the mob of Alexandria was so obsessed by hatred that it was by no means easy to call it off or to tear it from its prey.

---

[1] A distinguished Roman civil servant who was himself of Jewish origin. [ED.]
[2] The quarter in which the Jewish element was concentrated. [AUTHOR.]

THE RENEGADE
(A.D. 448)

(PRISCUS OF PANIUM: *History of His Own Times*: Teubner text = *Historici Graeci Minores*, ed. by L. Dindorf: Vol. I, pp. 305-309)[1]

NEXT morning, at dawn, Maximinus sent me to call upon Onegesius in order to present him with the gifts intended for him by Maximinus himself as well as those which had been sent by the Emperor. He was also anxious to ascertain the place and time at which Onegesius would be willing to grant him an interview. Accordingly, I put in an appearance with the attendants conveying the objects, and, finding the doors still closed, I tried to possess my soul in patience until somebody should emerge and announce our arrival. While I was waiting and pacing up and down in front of the enclosure surrounding the establishment, I was approached by an individual whom I presumed, from his nomad dress, to be a native, but who addressed me in Greek with the words "Good morning!"—a greeting which intrigued me, for here was good Greek issuing from the lips of a nomad. The nomads, being the sweepings of the earth, supplement their various vernaculars by some study of either Hunnish or Gothic or Latin (insofar as they have intercourse with the Romans),[2] while none of them readily speak Greek except the prisoners carried off from Thrace or from the Adriatic littoral. These unfortunates, however, were recognizable at sight. Their tattered clothing and unkempt heads signalized them as people who had come down in the world, whereas my friend had all the appearance of a prosperous nomad, with his smart clothes and his hair so neatly bobbed.

After returning his greeting, I inquired who he was and where he had lived before he had crossed into No-Man's-Land and adopted the nomadic life. He retorted by asking the motive of my eagerness to learn these details. I told him that the cause of my curiosity was his knowledge of Greek. Thereupon he laughed and told me that he was a Greek[3] by race who had

---

[1] The author was attached to a diplomatic mission dispatched in the year A.D. 448 by the Roman Government at Constantinople to Attila's headquarters in the Hungarian steppe, which is the scene of the incident here quoted. [ED.]

[2] Latin was at this time the language of all the Danubian Provinces of the Roman Empire from the Black Forest to the Black Sea, while Greek was hardly spoken north of the Balkan Range. [ED.]

[3] The author here uses the word Γραικὸς instead of Ἕλλην. [ED.]

come on business to the Moesian town of Viminacium[1] on the Danube. He had stayed there a long time, married a local heiress, and enjoyed a spell of prosperity; but he had been stripped of all this when the town fell into the hands of the tribesmen, on which occasion his former wealth had led to his being reserved for Onegesius himself in the division of the spoils. The well-to-do captives, he mentioned, were the special perquisite (after Attila had taken his choice) of the elite in the nomadic world, because they fetched the highest price when disposed of. However, he continued, he had distinguished himself in the subsequent actions against the Romans and against the Khazar[2] horde; had made over his winnings on active service to his native master, according to the nomadic regulations; and had thus obtained his freedom. He had married a native wife; he was the father of children; he was an honored guest at Onegesius's table; and he considered his present life preferable to his past.

Among the nomads, he explained, when the fighting was over you lived at ease; everybody was free to enjoy what he had in hand; and "live and let live" was the order of the day. Among the Romans it was a very different story. There in wartime, to begin with, it was easy to be wiped out when you trusted for your security to others than yourself, as you had to do because the despots set their veto upon universal service. As for the professional army, the cowardice of the superior officers, who were quite unequal to the rigors of war, was a greater danger than any. In peacetime, moreover, your experiences were more painful than the horrors of war itself owing to the merciless exaction of rates and taxes and the injuries inflicted by unprincipled members of the community upon their neighbors. The laws were not of universal application. If the offender belonged to the wealthy class, it was possible for him to evade punishment for his misconduct; whereas if he were a poor man without a knowledge of affairs he had to undergo the penalties which the law prescribed, unless, before sentence were delivered, he departed this life— as he well might do, considering the length of time to which suits were protracted and the vast sums consumed in costs. This, indeed, was perhaps the greatest grievance of all—this monetary charge for the privilege of obtaining your legal rights! Even the victim of injustice would not be awarded a true bill unless he paid down something for the benefit of the judge and his clerks.

When he held forth in this strain (at much greater length

[1] The modern Kostolatz in eastern Jugoslavia. [ED.]
[2] The name in the Greek text is uncertain. [ED.]

than I have reported him), I took up the challenge and mildly suggested that he ought to give a hearing to my side of the case. I proceeded to explain that the sagacious and high-principled statesmen who had created the Roman Constitution had sought to obviate social chaos by assigning the guardianship of the laws to some individuals and the supervision of armaments and responsibility for military efficiency to others, who were to have no other object set before them except to be prepared for action and to go on active service with as cool a courage as if it were ordinary maneuvers (which was not impossible when the instinct of fear had previously been eradicated by training). They had further assigned to individuals occupied in agriculture and in work on the land the task of maintaining the food supply—not only for themselves but for those who were fighting in their defense—a duty which they discharged by paying the *Army Food Stuffs Quota*. To others, again, they had assigned the function of protecting the victims of injustice—some of them by championing the cause of persons incapable, through lack of parts, of standing up for their own rights, and others (on the Bench) by seeing that the intention of the law was carried into effect. The interests of the litigants were not neglected, either, by the apparitors of the court, who included in their number officials whose duty it was to see that the party in whose favor judgment had been given obtained his rights, and equally that the party to whom the judgment was adverse was not distrained upon for a larger sum than had been fixed by decision of the court. If there were not officials to attend to these questions, the original case would always contain the germs of a second suit. Either the successful party would press his advantage too hard, or else the party discomfited in court would obstinately cling to his illegal point of view. All these servants of justice had been assigned a fixed rate of remuneration payable by the litigants, like the contribution payable by the agriculturists to the soldiers. Was it really so shocking that we should support our champions and make them some return for their benevolent attentions? It was the interest of the trooper to look after his mount; of the herdsman and the huntsman to take care of his cattle and his hounds respectively; and every class to provide for the particular fellow creatures to whom they owed their own maintenance and security. Litigants convicted with costs had no one but themselves and their own anti-social conduct to thank for their losses; and as for the undue protraction of suits, which might occasionally occur, this arose from an anxiety that justice should be done, and that the Bench should not fail to decide the case strictly on its merits through having

to deliver an offhand judgment. It was desirable that the
Bench should feel delay in winding up a case to be less ob-
jectionable than the consequences of precipitancy, which involved not merely injustice toward Man, but sin against the
Creator of justice, God. The laws were of universal application—so much so that they were obeyed by the Emperor himself—and there was no truth in the gravamen of his indictment, that the wealthy possessed impunity to overide the poor.
Improper acquittals were secured only by successful conceal-
ment of the offense, and this was of no more frequent occurrence in the case of the rich than in that of the poor, who
were equally exempt from being convicted for an offense in
the absence of sufficient evidence against them. Incidentally,
this was a universal phenomenon which was not confined to
the Roman world. As for the freedom which he had obtained,
he had to thank Fortune for that and not his nomad master
who, by taking him on active service, had exposed him to the
risk of destruction at the hands of the enemy through lack of
military experience or alternatively to that of punishment at
the hands of his owner for running away. The treatment of
slaves was, in fact, another field in which the Romans had
maintained their superiority. They behaved toward them like
fathers or teachers; used their influence to keep them from
bad habits and to inspire them with their own standards of
conduct; and corrected them for their faults as they would
their own children. Even over their slaves, the Romans did not
possess the power of life and death which was enjoyed by the
nomads; and in the Roman world there were many methods
of conferring freedom. The boon was granted not only during
the master's lifetime but also at his decease, in virtue of his
complete liberty of testamentary disposition. The Roman's
last will and testament in regard to his property was law.

My interlocutor was reduced to tears and confessed that the
laws were excellent and the Roman Constitution admirable,
if only the rulers had not so hopelessly lost the spirit of their
predecessors that they were ruining society. We were engaged
in this conversation when somebody came up from inside and
opened the doors of the enclosure.

PART II
CHARACTER

SECTION I—SOCIAL PSYCHOLOGY

DEMOCRACY

(HERODOTUS: Book V, chapters 78 and 97)

THE sovereign virtue of Democracy is demonstrated not only in a single particular but in a general way by the experience of the Athenians. Under despotic government the Athenians did not evince a military superiority over any of their neighbors, while they had no sooner got rid of their despots than they won by a long lead. This demonstrates that, so long as they were held down, they deliberately malingered out of a feeling that they were working for a master, whereas, after their liberation, each individual citizen felt the impulse to achieve victory for his own advantage.

     .   .   .   .   .

At this juncture, Aristagoras of Miletus, after being expelled from Sparta by Cleomenes the Lacedaemonian, arrived at Athens—the country which, after Sparta, was the greatest power in Hellas. Aristagoras was given a platform by the Athenian Assembly, where he repeated the representations which he had made at Sparta regarding the riches of Asia and Persian methods of warfare (his argument being that the Persians are not familiar with either shield or spear and would therefore be easy to conquer). He reinforced these points with the additional consideration that Miletus was a colony of Athens, and that Athens, being a great power, was under a moral obligation to protect the daughter country. There was nothing that he did not promise them in the vehemence of his entreaty, until eventually he won them over. Apparently it is a simpler matter to delude many individuals than one, considering that Aristagoras found himself unable to delude Cleomenes the Lacedaemonian in isolation, while he successfully accomplished the feat upon thirty thousand Athenians.

"PEACE TALK"
(425 B.C.)
(THUCYDIDES: Book IV, chapters 15-23, 27-28, and 40-41)

WHEN the news of what had happened at Pylos[1] arrived at Sparta, it was taken as a disaster of the first magnitude and the Assembly voted that the Government should visit the scene of operations and should be given a free hand to submit immediate proposals in the light of their personal observations. They soon saw that it was impossible to assist their comrades, and they were unwilling to run the risk of their suffering extremities of famine or being overwhelmed by force of numbers. They therefore decided to prevail, if possible, upon the Athenian commanders to conclude an armistice at Pylos and then to send a diplomatic mission to Athens to arrange a settlement, with a view to the earliest possible recovery of their beleaguered countrymen. The Athenian commanders accepted the proposal and an armistice was arranged on the following terms: The Lacedaemonians were to assemble at Pylos and deliver to the Athenians not only the ships which they had brought into action but all ships of fighting build in Laconia, and they were not to attack the fortified post either by land or by sea. The Athenians, on their side, were to allow the Lacedaemonians on the mainland to supply their comrades in the island with a stated ration of cereals[2] ready-kneaded, but this was to be landed under Athenian control and there was to be no attempt at blockade running. The Athenians were to blockade the island as actively as before, except that they were not to send landing parties ashore and not to attack the Peloponnesian forces either by land or by sea. If either party broke any of these conditions in any respect, then the armistice was to lapse automatically. Otherwise, it was to hold until the return from Athens of the Lacedaemonian mission, whom the Athenians were to transport, both going and coming, on a warship. Upon their return, the present armistice was automatically to lapse, and the Athenians were to restore the ships in the condition in which they had received them. These

---

[1] An Athenian naval squadron had established a fortified post in the ancient castle of Pylos on the west coast of Laconia, and had afterward cut off 420 Lacedaemonian infantry who had been stationed on the neighboring island of Sphacteria during the resulting operations. [ED.]

[2] Two Attic quarts of barley meal per infantryman, with two pints of wine and a portion of meat. Servants were to be allowed half-rations. [AUTHOR.]

were the terms on which the armistice was concluded, whereupon the ships were delivered, to the number of something
like sixty, and the mission was dispatched. Upon their arrival
at Athens, they delivered the following *note verbale*:

"Gentlemen, our country has sent us, on behalf of our
comrades on the island, to negotiate any arrangement which
we can demonstrate to your satisfaction to be in the interests
of Athens and which will at the same time enable us to retrieve
our disaster with the least derogation to our honor—considering the situation in which we find ourselves. If we enlarge
somewhat fully upon the objects of our mission, that will not
be a breach of our national custom; for while it is our tradition
to avoid diffuseness where brevity suffices, it is equally our
tradition to expand whenever an occasion arises for making an
important exposition and when words are the most effective
instruments of action. Do not receive our note in a hostile
spirit and do not take our exposition as an insult to your intelligence. Treat what we have to tell you as an *aide memoire*
addressed to an audience which has anticipated for itself the
suggestions therein tendered.

"An opportunity is now presented to you of reaping full
advantage from your present success by keeping what you hold
and keeping it with honor and glory, instead of reacting as
human beings do when they secure a prize without being ac-
customed to the experience. In this situation, the hope excited
by the windfall of the moment invariably entices them into
grasping after more, whereas their fellows who have expe-
rienced a series of vicissitudes, bad as well as good, would
properly view any success with profound suspicion. If extent
of experience is the test, then logically our country and yours
should be better endowed with this quality of skepticism than
any others; and if you require an object lesson, you have only
to turn your gaze upon the present disasters of Lacedaemon
and to realize that we, who now stand at your door, are the
power possessed of the greatest prestige in Hellas—a power
which previously regarded itself as in a stronger position to
offer the very terms which we have now come to ask you. It
is significant that our mishap cannot be traced to any inadequacy in our power or to any loss of mental balance due to
its aggrandizement. Our resources are what they always have
been and our error is an error of judgment, to which all human
beings are equally exposed. It would therefore be irrational on
your part if the actual strength, at this moment, of your country and its recent accessions were to lead you into imagining
that Fortune will always work in your favor. The only safe
way to dispose of success is to treat it as precarious, and that
is precisely what wise men do and what enables wise men to

show better judgment in facing disasters. Similarly, the only safe way to treat war is to realize that you cannot confine your dealings with it within the particular limits that happen to suit your fancy, but that the initiative lies in the hands of Fortune. Men imbued with this wisdom are not naïvely elated by the tide of military success. They therefore escape with the minimum number of reverses and are readiest to make peace at the maximum point in their success.

"You, gentlemen, have an admirable opportunity now of practicing this wisdom toward us. Do so, and you will have ruled out forever the numerous possibilities of catastrophe which may overtake you if you do otherwise and which may expose you to the imputation that even your recent successes have been thrust into your hands by Fortune. Why take this risk, when it is open to you to bequeath to posterity an unassailable reputation for strength and insight?

"Lacedaemon invites you to an armistice for the termination of the war. She offers you peace and alliance and the most extensive and intimate relations of friendship in every sphere. She asks in return for the restoration of her sons on the island, because she considers it better for both parties that they should not decide by force of arms the question whether the besieged might be enabled by some favorable turn of Fortune to break through to safety or whether (as is more likely) the defense would be overpowered and would end in their reduction. In our belief, the best hope of composing the great quarrels of the world by permanent reconciliations is not to be found in the philosophy of retaliation and of military triumph and of the extortion, under *force majeure*, of signatures to an imposed and inequitable settlement. No! That hope arises when the victor renounces these his privileges in order to show himself a victor in the nobler field of generosity and to astonish his adversary by the moderation of his terms. That gesture breaks the chain of retaliations, challenges the other party to requite generosity in kind, and enlists his conscience in favor of abiding by his covenant. Now human beings find it easier to show this magnanimity to a deadly enemy than to those with whom they are in moderate disagreement, and human nature delights in meeting voluntary concessions in the spirit in which they are made, whereas it insists upon resisting presumptuousness to the death, however desperate the prospect.

"For our own two countries, the present moment is the most opportune possible for effecting a reconciliation. So far, we have escaped without any irremediable incident coming between us to drive Lacedaemonians into what would be a personal as well as a political feud against Athenians to all eternity, and a feud which would close to Athens the door

which we now invite her to enter. Let us come to terms while
the decision is still in suspense—terms which will confer glory
and the friendship of Sparta upon you, while they will enable
us to avoid disgrace by compounding for a disaster on tolerable
conditions. Let us make the choice of peace instead of war for
ourselves, and the choice of a respite from their troubles for
our fellow Hellenes. In this momentous issue Hellas will charge
Athens with the heavier responsibility. She knows not whether
you or we began the war in which she finds herself involved,
but if peace is made—which rests in your hands more than in
ours—she will make you the recipient of her gratitude. The
permanent friendship of Lacedaemon will likewise be at your
command if you take this decision, and Lacedaemon will have
made the first advance to an Athens who has not imposed her
will but has conferred a favor. It is impossible to exaggerate
the potential advantages of such a solution. Athens and Sparta
have only to agree and you know well that the rest of the
Hellenic world will recognize our superiority and will respect
us in proportion."

The Lacedaemonians delivered this speech in the belief that
the Athenians had for some time been anxious for an armistice
and had only been frustrated by Lacedaemonian opposition,
so that when peace was offered they would accept it thank-
fully and restore the beleaguered men. The Athenians, however, took the view that, with the enemy trapped on the island,
an armistice was henceforward at their disposal whenever
they chose to conclude it, and with this view they grasped after
more. Their evil genius was Cleon, son of Cleaenetus, a politician of the day who exercised an extraordinary influence over
the masses; and Cleon now induced the Assembly to reply
that first of all the troops on the island must surrender their
arms and their persons and be conveyed to Athens, and that
after their arrival the Lacedaemonians must restore Nisaea and
Pegae and Trozen and Achaea[1] before recovering their men
and obtaining a peace to run for whatever period might be
agreeable to the two parties. To this answer the Lacedaemonian mission made no reply, but suggested the appointment of a
committee to sit with them in order to arrive in due course at
a negotiated settlement by a full discussion of the points at
issue. At this, Cleon went off in full cry. All along, he declared,
he had divined their dishonest intentions, and now they were
as clear as day when they refused to make any statement to
the masses and proposed a conference with one or two indi-

[1] These territories had not been conquered by the Lacedaemonians by force of
arms, but had been surrendered by the Athenians under the previous treaty of
peace [446 B.C.], at a moment of disaster at which they had been in greater need
of peace than the Lacedaemonians. [AUTHOR.]

viduals. If their intentions were honorable, he challenged them to state them to the Assembly.

The Lacedaemonians realized that it was impossible for them to announce in public any concessions which the disaster might conceivably have induced them to offer, for fear that an announcement followed by a rejection might destroy their prestige with their allies, and they realized equally that the Athenians would not respond to their overtures on any tolerable conditions. They therefore left Athens with their mission unaccomplished. Immediately upon their return the armistice at Pylos automatically lapsed and the Lacedaemonians proceeded to reclaim their ships according to the agreement. The Athenians, however, seized the excuse of a raid against the fortified post in violation of the armistice and of other flagrantly trivial incidents in order to refuse to restore them, insisting upon the undoubted text of the agreement to the effect that the armistice would lapse automatically in the event of any infringement whatsoever. The Lacedaemonians protested against their conduct in regard to the ships, which they stigmatized as an outrage, and settled down to hostilities, with the result that the operations at Pylos were actively resumed on either side.

.   .   .   .   .   .

At Athens, the news that the force [at Pylos] was in distress and that provisions were arriving by sea for the beleaguered detachment on the island created perplexity and aroused a fear that the blockade might be overtaken by winter. They foresaw the impossibility of transporting supplies round the Peloponnese, considering that Pylos itself produced nothing and that even in summer they had been unable to send round cargoes in sufficient quantities. Then also foresaw that on this harborless coast they could not maintain their naval cordon, and that if the detachment did not escape through the abandonment of the blockade, they would watch for bad weather and put off in the boats which had been bringing them their provisions. They were most disturbed of all at the attitude of the Lacedaemonian Government who must, they imagined, have some strong ground to account for their omission to pursue their overtures. In fact, the Athenians began to repent of having rejected the armistice proposals, and Cleon, realizing the misgivings now aroused by his action in frustrating a settlement, attempted to give the lie to the individuals who brought the reports. The latter, however, suggested that if the Assembly did not believe their word, they should send a commission of inquiry, whereupon the Assembly appointed as commissioner Cleon himself, with Theägenes for his colleague. Cleon at once realized that he would be forced either to confirm the reports of the individuals whom he had libeled or to contradict them at the cost of being exposed as a liar, and he perceived at the same time that the Assembly were more inclined than not to carry on the operations. He therefore suggested that it would be a mistake to waste precious time by sending commissioners, and that if they believed in the truth of the reports they ought to sail against the enemy. He then attempted to reflect upon Nicias, son of Nicērătus, one of the generals of the year, whose enemy he was, with the censorious remark that, if the generals were men, it was easy to sail with a proper force and to capture the detachment on the island, and that this was what he would have done had he been in office himself. Nicias, encouraged by hearing cries of shame against Cleon for not sailing anyhow, if it seemed to him so easy, and at the same time provoked by Cleon's censorious tone, requested Cleon to take whatever force he liked and to attempt the operation with the Government's blessing. Cleon, who imagined at first that he was not in earnest, professed his readiness, only to discover that Nicias's anxiety to hand over was genuine—whereupon he attempted to draw back and protested that Nicias was general and not he. He was now in a panic, having never imagined that Nicias would venture to retire in his favor. Nicias proceeded to repeat his request, to renounce the command at Pylos, and to call the Assembly to witness, and the Assembly displayed the habitual psychology of the crowd. The more Cleon shrank from the expedition and tried to back out of what he had said, the more they encouraged Nicias to hand over the command and clamored at Cleon to sail. At last, not seeing how to slip out of what he had said, Cleon undertook the expedition. Rising to speak, he declared that he was not afraid of the Lacedaemonians and that he would not take with him one man from the home country but only the Lemnians[1] and Imbrians[1] who were at Athens, a body of mercenary light infantry from Aenus[2] and four hundred archers recruited elsewhere. With this reinforcement to the troops already at Pylos, he promised to bring the Lacedaemonians to Athens as prisoners within three weeks, or else to exterminate them on the scene of action. The Assembly could not help laughing at his fatuity, but the sensible portion of the public derived satisfaction from the thought that they would gain in either event. Either they would be rid of Cleon, which they considered more likely, or their disappointment would be compensated by the reduction of the Lacedaemonians. Cleon carried all his requirements in the Assembly, which

---

[1] Athenian colonists. [Ed.]
[2] A Hellenic town in Eastern Thrace at the mouth of the River Maritsa. [Ed.]

voted him the command of the expedition. He chose a single
colleague from among the commanders at Pylos in the person
of Demosthenes, and pushed forward the preparations for his
voyage.

.   .   .   .

Cleon's insane promise came true, for he brought the enemy
to Athens as prisoners within three weeks, as he had undertaken to do, although no event in the late war took Hellas so
much by surprise as this. It had been assumed that neither
hunger nor any other form of pressure would induce the Lacedaemonians to capitulate, but that they would fight on as best
they could and die weapons in hand. It seemed incredible that
those who surrendered should be of the same clay as the fallen,
and at a later date the question was put to one of the prisoners
by a national of some Allied state of Athens in the deliberately
wounding form: "Were the fallen men of honor?" The answer
was: "One would give a great deal for a shaft[1] that could distinguish men of honor"—indicating that the execution done
by the stones and missiles had been indiscriminate.

When the prisoners arrived at Athens, the Assembly decided to keep them in rigorous confinement until the conclusion of peace and to lead them out to execution if the Peloponnesians invaded Attic territory in the interval. The defense
of Pylos was provided for, and the Messenians of Naupactus[2]
sent their likeliest men to what they regarded as their home
country.[3] The fact that these Messenians spoke the local dialect
rendered the raids which they started in Laconia peculiarly
destructive. The Lacedaemonians had no previous experience
of brigandage and guerrilla warfare, and the desertions on the
part of the serfs, coupled with the fear of some more extensive revolutionary movement in the country, were so trying to
their endurance that, in spite of their anxiety not to betray
their state of mind to the Athenians, they began to send missions to Athens and to negotiate for the restoration of Pylos
and the prisoners. The Athenians, however, kept grasping after
more, and dismissed mission after mission with their object
unaccomplished.

[1] *I.e.,* "arrow." [AUTHOR.]
[2] Survivors of the serf revolt in Laconia of 464 B.C. The insurgents had eventually capitulated to the Spartan Government on condition of withdrawing from
Laconian territory and had been settled by the Athenian Government at their
new naval station of Naupactus in the Corinthian Gulf. [ED.]
[3] Pylos is situated in the former territory of Messenia. [AUTHOR.]

"MORALE"

(401 B.C.)

(XENOPHON: *The Expedition of Cyrus*: Book III, chapter 1, sections 2-4 and 11-47)[1]

AFTER the arrest of the generals and the massacre of the officers and privates who had accompanied them, the Hellenes were in the depths of despair. They were tormented by the thought that they were at the Great King's doors; that they were surrounded in every direction by a host of unfriendly nations and towns; that nobody would any longer be willing to sell them supplies; that they were separated by a distance of at least twelve or thirteen hundred miles from Hellas; that they had no guide to show them the way; that their homeward road was intersected and blocked by impassable rivers; that their Oriental comrades on the expedition had betrayed them; and that they were left in isolation without a single cavalryman on their side, which made it as clear as day that when they were successful they would inflict no casualties, whereas when they suffered a reverse they would be annihilated. These thoughts so disheartened them that few of them tasted food at nightfall and few lighted campfires, while numbers did not go that night to their quarters but remained off duty wherever they happened to find themselves—though they could not sleep for misery and out of homesickness for their countries, parents, wives, and children, whom they never expected to see again. This was the state of mind in which they all remained off duty.

Among the members of the army there was a certain Xenophon of Athens who had joined the strength without the rank of either general or company commander or private. He had left his home on the special invitation of Proxenus, who was his family friend[2] and who had promised, if he came, to in-

[1] Cyrus the Younger, the Persian viceroy of Western Anatolia, had rebelled against his elder brother, King Artaxerxes II, and had marched from the coast of the Aegean Sea upcountry in order to seize the throne. Besides his Oriental troops, he had recruited (in round numbers) 10,000 Hellenic mercenaries from among the mass of Hellenes who found themselves unemployed or in exile at the close of the Peloponnesian War. The two brothers met at Cunaxa in 'Iraq, where the victory of Cyrus's Hellenes was transformed into a virtual defeat by the death of Cyrus on the battlefield. The Ten Thousand, who had now lost both their employer and their objective, started to retreat in company with their Oriental comrades, and the two forces made a compact of mutual fidelity. After a few marches, however, Cyrus's Oriental followers secretly came to terms with King Artaxerxes and inveigled the generals of the Hellenic force into a conference at the headquarters of the King's army of observation, where the Hellenic generals were treacherously arrested and their attendants massacred. [ED.]

[2] Proxenus of Boeotia was one of the condottieri who had raised the force for Cyrus and had now been arrested with his colleagues. [ED.]

troduce him to Cyrus, and Cyrus (Proxenus declared) meant more to Proxenus himself than home and country . . .[1] Now that despair had descended upon the army, Xenophon was as miserable as the rest and was unable to sleep, but in dozing off for a moment he had a dream. He fancied that it thundered and that a thunderbolt fell upon his family home, which was all lighted up by it. Instantly he awoke in a fright, and interpreted the dream as being good in one sense, inasmuch as, in the midst of trouble and danger, he had fancied that he saw a great light from Zeus, though in another sense he was alarmed because he fancied that the source of the dream was Zeus the King and that the light from the fire shone in a ring, which suggested that he might not succeed in escaping from the King's country but might be hemmed in by various obstacles in every direction. However, the true significance of this class of dream may be discerned from the sequel, which was as follows. The first thing that happened to Xenophon, immediately after he awoke, was that he was struck by a thought: "Why am I lying inactive while the night is passing, when dawn will presumably bring the enemy down upon us? If we fall into the King's power, what will stand between us and a shameful death accompanied by all the most hideous experiences and the most exquisite tortures? And yet nobody is organizing or superintending any plan of resistance, but here we are lying inactive as though we could afford to be idle. Take myself. To what other nation am I looking for a general to act for me? What age am I waiting to reach before I act for myself? In my case, I shall never be a day older than I am, if today I betray myself into the hands of the enemy." At that point Xenophon got up and called together in the first instance the company commanders of Proxenus's regiment, to whom he gave the following address as soon as they had assembled:

"Personally, gentlemen, I can neither sleep—as I imagine that you cannot either—nor can I lie inactive any longer, considering our position. The enemy have obviously waited to make open war upon us until they considered that they had prepared themselves satisfactorily for eventualities, yet no one on our side is taking counter-measures to insure that we shall give the best possible account of ourselves. At the same time, if we give in and fall into the King's power, what treatment do we expect to receive? What did the King do to his own mother's son, and that after he was dead? He cut off his head and hand and crucified his body, and here are we who have no protector to stand by us and who have marched against the

---

[1] The author's note on his doubts at the time as to whether he should accept the invitation, and on his consultation of Socrates, has been omitted. [Ed.]

King in order to degrade him from sovereign to slave—if we did not succeed in taking his life! What treatment have we to expect? Undoubtedly the King will go to extremes in his determination to inflict such appalling horrors upon us that nobody in the world will ever venture to march against him in future. Therefore, surely, we must avoid falling into his power *at all costs*. Personally, so long as the armistice lasted, I never ceased to be sorry for ourselves and envious of the King and his court, when I surveyed their position and saw the extent and fertility of their country, the abundance of their supplies, and the multitude of their servants and their livestock and all the gold and all the finery. On the contrary, whenever I thought over the position of our troops, and remembered that we had not a right to one particle of this richness unless we paid for it, whereas I knew that all but a few of us had already emptied our purses and that we were now debarred by treaty from providing ourselves with supplies by any method except purchase—why, the thoughts that I have confessed to you sometimes made me more afraid of the armistice than I am now afraid of war. Now that the enemy have broken the armistice, the foundations of their superciliousness and of our uneasiness have, in my opinion, been broken up by their act. All this richness has been thrown into the arena, as a prize for whichever of us prove ourselves the better men; and the umpires are the gods, to whose support we may reasonably look forward. Why so? Because the enemy have perjured themselves in the gods' name, whereas we have so scrupulously respected our oath that we have rigidly kept our hands off the immense riches which we saw before our eyes. This justifies us, in my opinion, in entering upon the struggle with a far greater measure of self-confidence than our opponents. Besides, we are constitutionally fitter than they are to stand extremes of heat and cold and fatigue, while by the grace of the gods we are as much their superiors in spirit; and, lastly, these people are more vulnerable—and mortally vulnerable—than we, if the gods give us the victory as they have done hitherto. In all probability these very ideas are occurring at this moment to our comrades, and, that being so, in Heaven's name do not let us wait for others to approach us with the summons to the field of honor. Let us be the first to stimulate our comrades to show their mettle. Prove yourselves the best officers in the army and fitter for command than the generals themselves. Personally, if you desire to take the initiative, I am ready to follow you, while, if you depute me to take the lead, I will not excuse myself on grounds of age. I feel perfectly in my prime for fighting for my existence."

After listening to Xenophon's address, the officers requested him to take the lead unanimously, except for a certain Apollonides who talked with a Boeotian accent. This individual declared that it was nonsense to say that there was any loophole of escape except through doing their best to mollify the King, and he at once began to retail the difficulties. Xenophon, however, interrupted him with the following apostrophe:

"I am perfectly amazed at you, sir. Your trouble is that you are incapable of being impressed by the evidence of your senses. After all, you were present with our comrades here at the moment when, after Cyrus's death, the King was so set up that he sent us orders to surrender our arms. Now when, instead of surrendering them, we put them on and planted our camp next door to His Majesty's, did he leave one stone unturned in the way of sending *parlementaires* and begging for an armistice and providing supplies until at last he had obtained his armistice from us? On the other hand, when the generals and company commanders did what you would have us do now and went unarmed to parley with the enemy in reliance upon the armistice, are they not at this very moment being beaten and stabbed and outraged without even being able, poor fellows, to die, though I imagine that that is the release for which they are longing? Knowing all this, as you do, you dismiss the proposal to fight as nonsense, and you propose instead that we should go a second time to—mollify the King! Personally, gentlemen, I move that we boycott this creature, degrade him from his command, and saddle him with the baggage as the best employment for him. He is a disgrace to his country and a disgrace to all Hellas—to be a Hellene and to behave as he is doing!" This was immediately followed up by Agasias of Stymphalus, who remarked: "As a matter of fact, the creature has no connection with Boeotia or with Hellas whatsoever. I have seen for myself that he has both his ears pierced like a Lydian!" This was a fact, so the creature was driven away and the others started to pass along the lines and to call up the officers—the general, where he still survived; the lieutenant general in units where the general had been lost; and, where a company commander survived, the company commander. When they had all assembled, they took their seats to the front of the bivouacs, the total number of generals and company commanders reporting being about a hundred. By this time it was nearly midnight. Thereupon Hieronymus of Elis, the senior company commander in Proxenus's regiment, opened the proceedings as follows: "In our regiment, gentlemen, we have decided, in view of the situation, to hold a meeting ourselves and to invite you to join us, in the hope that we may be able to find some good plan of action. I now call upon Xenophon to say again to the meeting what he has already said to us." After this introduction, Xenophon spoke to the following effect:

"There is one thing of which we are all aware, and that is that the King and Tissaphernes[1] have arrested as many of us as they could and are obviously intriguing against the rest, in order to destroy us if they can do so. Our own business, in my opinion, is *at all costs* to avoid falling into the Orientals' power, and to take care that, if anything, it shall be they who fall into ours. Now you know better than I can tell you that those present at this meeting have, between them, an immense opportunity in their hands. All the troops are looking to you and, if they see you downhearted, every man of them will fail in his duty. On the other hand, if you make it apparent that you are organizing resistance to the enemy on your own account, and if you call upon the rest to support you, you know very well that they will follow you and will do their best to act up to your example. May it not, in fact, be no more than right that you should be better men than your subordinates? You are generals, battalion commanders, company commanders, and in peacetime you enjoyed advantages which your troops did not, in the way of pay and distinctions. Well, now it is wartime, and, that being so, you may fairly be called upon to show yourselves better men, man for man, than the rank and file, and to employ your wits and exert your bodies on their behalf in all eventualities. To start with the first step, I think that you would do the Army a great service if you made immediate arrangements for the replacement of the lost generals and company commanders. Without leaders, there is no possibility of good or satisfactory results. That is broadly true in every sphere, and in soldiering it is true without exception. Everything shows that Discipline is Salvation, while indiscipline has been the historic grave of armies. As soon as you have appointed the necessary number of officers, I think you would be doing just what the situation demands if you paraded the troops and gave them some encouragement. Probably you have noticed already for yourselves how downhearted they were—downhearted when they went to their quarters and downhearted on sentry duty. In fact, in their present condition, I cannot conceive their being anything but useless, either for night operations or by daylight. If somebody can divert their minds from dwelling exclusively upon what is going to happen to them and induce them, instead, to think of what they are going to do, that will put vastly more heart into them. You know, I am sure, that neither numbers nor strength are the

[1] Former governor general of one of the provinces (the modern vilayet of Aidin) which had been included in Cyrus's viceroyalty, and therefore Cyrus's mortal enemy. [ED.]

secret of military victory, but that whichever side by the gods' help shows the stouter heart in attacking the enemy nearly always finds that the other side does not wait to face them. There is another thought, gentlemen, that has planted itself in my mind, and that is that the soldier who seeks at any price to save his life is nearly always the soldier who ineffectively and disgracefully loses it, whereas the man who has made up his mind that death is the common and inevitable lot of mankind, and who throws all his energies into dying with glory, is on the whole, in my experience, the man who comes to a good old age and who, while life lasts, enjoys his life the most thoroughly. That is just the text for our present situation. Take it to heart, gentlemen; show yourselves brave men; and ask the same of your comrades."

These concluding words of Xenophon's were followed by a few from Cheirisophus: "Xenophon, up to now my acquaintance with you has been confined to hearing that you were an Athenian,[1] but now I pay you my homage for what you are saying and doing, and I could only wish that we had as many Xenophons as possible. The more of them, the better for all. And now, gentlemen, there is no time to be lost, so go back at once and elect officers where needed, and, when you have elected them, report at headquarters with the men of your choice, and then we will parade the troops there. Notify Tolmides, the herald, to attend." Before he had finished speaking he had risen to his feet, in order that no time should be lost in executing the program, and thereupon the following leaders were chosen: in Clearchus's place, Timasion of Dardanus; in Socrates's, Xanthicles of Achaea; in Agias's, Cleänor of Arcadia; in Meno's, Philesius of Achaea; and in Proxenus's, Xenophon of Athens.

"THE SEA! THE SEA!"

(XENOPHON: *The Expedition of Cyrus*: Book IV, chapter 7, sections 19-27)

FROM there[2] they covered four marches totaling twenty *farsakhs,* which brought them to a prosperous and well-populated town called Gymnias. From this point the local chief sent the Hellenes a guide in order to conduct them across the territory

---

[1] Cheirisophus was a Spartan and the Peloponnesian War had only ended four years before. [ED.]

[2] By this time the Ten Thousand had made their way northward from 'Iraq through Northern Kurdistan and Armenia until they had reached the neighborhood of the Black Sea in the modern vilayet of Trebizond. [ED.]

of hostile neighbors. The guide presented himself and stated that in five days he would bring them to a place with a view of the sea. He staked his life on being as good as his word. He guided the Army so as to violate the hostile territory and then urged them to burn and devastate the country, which made it as clear as daylight that this was his object in coming and not any good will toward the Hellenes. They duly arrived at the crest of the mountain[1] on the fifth day, and when the leading files found themselves on the crest and caught sight of the sea there was an immense uproar. When Xenophon and the rearguard heard the noise, they imagined that a second hostile force must be attacking the vanguard.[2] The shouting, however, steadily increased in volume and came nearer; one file after another broke into the double to join their shouting comrades; and the noise grew louder as the numbers increased, until Xenophon felt at last that it must be something serious. He accordingly mounted and started to pass up the column, in support, with Lycius and the cavalry, when it was not long before they heard the soldiers shouting "The Sea! The Sea!" and passing the word along. At that, the whole force went off at the double, rearguard and all, with the mule train at full gallop as well as the horses. When at last they had all arrived at the summit, what should they do but embrace each other and their generals and their company commanders with tears in their eyes. Then suddenly somebody passed the word and the troops gathered stones until they had made a great pile. This they proceeded to decorate with a quantity of raw oxhides and truncheons and the captured shields, and the guide took the lead in cutting up the shields and called on the others to copy him. After this the guide was sent home by the Hellenes, but first they presented him in the name of the Army with a horse and a silver goblet and a Persian equipment and ten gold pieces. The guide asked specially for finger rings, of which he received a large quantity from the troops. He showed them a village in which to bivouac and the road which was to take them into the country of the Macrōnes and then, when evening came, he went off in the dark.

---

[1] The name of this mountain was Thēchēs. [AUTHOR.]

[2] Enemy from the burning villages were hanging on their rear, and the rearguard had inflicted some casualties upon these, and taken some prisoners, as the result of an ambush. About twenty wicker-and-rawhide shields remained in their hands. The hides were those of long-haired cattle. [AUTHOR.]

LIBERATION
(196 B.C.)

(PLUTARCH: *Parallel Lives*: Teubner text, ed. by C. Sintenis, Vol. II: *Titus Quinctius Flamininus*, chapter 10)

THE Board of Ten Commissioners sent by the Senate to advise Titus[1] had made the recommendation that all Hellas should be liberated with the exception of Corinth, Chalcis, and Demetrias, but that Roman garrisons should be retained in these three fortresses as a precaution against Antiochus.[2] At this news, the Aetolians[3] began to shatter the nerves of Hellas with shrill denunciations. They called upon Titus to release Hellas from her "Fetters."[4] They asked the Hellenes whether the smoother but heavier collar which they were now wearing was a satisfactory exchange for the old one, and whether they reverenced Titus as a benefactor for having taken the shackles off Hellas's feet in order to imprison her neck in them. This attack so vexed and mortified Titus that he appealed to the Commissioners, until at length he succeeded in persuading them to exempt these three towns, as well, from the imposition of garrisons, in order that his generosity to Hellas might be perfect and entire.

The Isthmian Games[5] were being held, and the stadium was packed with spectators watching the athletic competitions, as was natural now that Hellas had found release, at last, from her long wars in pursuit of liberty and was celebrating an unmistakable peace in high festival. Suddenly, the signal for general silence was given by a blast on the trumpet, and the herald advanced into the arena to make the following proclamation: "The Senate of Rome and Titus Quinctius, Consul and General in Chief,[6] in virtue of their decisive victory over King Philip and the Government of Macedonia, hereby re-

[1] As a result of the Battle of Cynoscephalae (197 B.C.), in which the Romans under Flamininus had defeated King Philip V of Macedonia, the latter country had ceded to Rome all her possessions on Hellenic soil south of the Pass of Tempe, and the Roman Government had now to decide how to dispose of them. [ED.]

[2] Antiochus III of the Seleucid Dynasty. The center of his power lay southeast of the Taurus, but he was at this time reasserting the claims of his predecessors to territories in Anatolia and Thrace. [ED.]

[3] The Aetolian Confederation had been in alliance with Rome in the war against Macedonia; but, as often happens, the relations between the Allies were suffering under the strain of too complete an overthrow of the common enemy. [ED.]

[4] As Philip had been in the habit of calling the three places aforementioned. [AUTHOR.]

[5] They were held, once in every four years, on the Isthmus, in the territory of Corinth. [ED.]

[6] "General in Chief" was the technical paraphrase, in Greek, for the Latin "Consul," the simple word "General" being employed for the Latin "Praetor." [ED.]

lease from all military occupation, all political interference, all exaction of tribute, and all infringement of their national institutions the states of Corinth, Locris, Phocis, Euboea, Achaea Phthiotis, Magnesia, Thessaly, and Perrhaebia." At the first moment, the words were not heard distinctly by the whole audience. The stadium surged with tumultuous and bewildered inquiries and with demands for a second reading. When silence had been restored, the herald once more recited the proclamation—this time in louder tones and with a greater effort to render it audible to all his hearers—and then a mighty cheer re-echoed, in an incredible volume of joyful sound, from the stadium to the sea. The entire audience had risen to its feet; the performances were forgotten; and every spectator was straining on tiptoe to greet with hand and voice the Savior and Champion of Hellas.

PUBLIC OPINION
(171 B.C.)
(POLYBIUS: Book XXVII, chapters 9-10)

AFTER the Macedonian victory, the story of the cavalry engagement[1] spread through Hellas, whereupon public opinion in regard to Perseus, which had previously refrained almost completely from declaring itself, blazed out like fire. I will try to explain my notion of what this opinion was. The phenomenon was a close parallel to what occurs in athletic competitions. Whenever in such cases a celebrated champion with the reputation of invincibility is challenged by an obscure antagonist who is a markedly weaker competitor, the crowd at once bestows its sympathy upon the weaker party, cheers him, and cannot contain itself in its partisanship on his behalf. If he so much as touches his opponent's face and leaves any mark of the blow, immediately the spectators are all on tenterhooks of expectancy.[2] Sometimes they actually go so far as to hoot the other competitor—not because they hate him or think badly of him, but in an irrational outburst of sensibility which makes them bestow their sympathy upon the weaker physique. On the other hand, if pulled up in time they rapidly change round and are not long in grasping their own stupidity.

There is a story that the crowd was so handled by Clito-

[1] One of the first engagements in the Third Romano-Macedonian War (171-168 B.C.), in which the Romans had suffered a reverse, though the war eventually resulted in the fall of the Macedonian Monarchy. [ED.]

[2] The original Greek text of this sentence is so corrupt that the translation is conjectural. [ED.]

machus, an athlete who was supposed to hold the championship in his profession and who was therefore a popular celeb-
rity all over the world. The story is that King Ptolemy set his
heart upon destroying Clītomachus's reputation and displayed
the utmost keenness in training the boxer Aristonīcus, whose
physique was thought to be superlatively good for the particular purpose, in order to enter him against the champion.
When Aristonicus presented himself in Hellas and challenged
Clitomachus at Olympia, it appears that the crowd forthwith
transferred their backing to Aristonicus and gave him their
cheers, in their delight that somebody had ventured for one
moment to challenge Clitomachus. When Aristonicus proceeded to show himself a match for his opponent in the actual
fight and delivered one or two telling blows, there was a thun-
der of applause and the majority of the spectators could not
contain themselves in their partisanship for Aristonicus, whom
they cheered to the echo. On this occasion Clitomachus apparently stepped out of the ring for a moment's breathing space
and then turned upon the crowd and asked them what they
meant by cheering Aristonicus and siding with him in every way
in their power. Could they honestly say that he (Clitomachus)
was not playing the game, or did they not realize that while
he himself was in this fight for the honor of Hellas, Aristonicus
was in it for the sake of His Majesty King Ptolemy? Which
did they prefer? That an Egyptian subject should carry off
the Olympia Wreath for having won it from the Hellenes, or
that a Boeotian from Thebes should be proclaimed the winner
in the Adult Boxing Championship? These remarks of Clitomachus's are said to have produced such an extreme revul-
sion of feeling among the majority of the spectators that the
positions were reversed and that the crowd did more than
Clitomachus himself toward knocking Aristonicus out.

The behavior of public opinion in the case of Perseus was a
close parallel to my story. If anyone had pulled the public up
and had asked them frankly whether they would really like
to see such an overwhelming ascendency accrue to a single
individual[1] and would really like to learn the meaning of a
monarchical regime which would be absolute in every sense,
I imagine that they would very soon have come to their senses,
made their recantation, and swung over to the opposite extreme. In fact, in my belief it would only have been necessary
to recall a few instances of the harsh treatment of Hellas by
the House of Macedonia and of her considerate treatment at
the hands of Rome in order to produce in the public mind a
paroxysm of repentance. However, at the moment in question
the first unconsidered impulse of public opinion betrayed an

---

[1] As would accrue to Perseus if he won the war. [Ed.]

unmistakable satisfaction at the news [of the Macedonian success], the source of the pleasure being the miracle that anybody at all should have shown himself capable of standing up to the Romans. My motive in enlarging upon this point has been to shield Hellas from uncritical but damaging accusations of ingratitude for the behavior of public opinion on this occasion—accusations which could only be made in ignorance of the facts of psychology.

IN THE THEATER AT ASCULUM
(91 B.C.)

(DIODORUS: *Library of Universal History*: ed. by C. Müller, Paris, 1844, Didot, Vol. II; and by L. Dindorf, Leipzig, 1868, Teubner, Vol. V: Book XXXVII, fragment 12)

THERE happened to be a round of performances and the theater[1] was full of Roman citizens who had turned up as spectators,[2] when an artist was assassinated in the theater while actually performing on the stage, because his acting was supposed[3] to be out of keeping with the gravity of the crisis. In a moment the mask of festivity revealed the grim features of war; there was an agony of panic; and then Fortune came to the rescue with a piece of comic relief, in the shape of the humorist Saunio. This personage, who held the Latin franchise,[4] possessed an extraordinary gift for drollery. He could not only make people laugh when he talked, but the slightest wriggle of his body fetched a smile from his audience without his having to speak a word. There was something about his personality that was irresistible, and any Roman audience might be relied upon to give him a tremendous reception. The Confederates determined to deprive the Romans of this innocent enjoyment by killing the poor producer of it; but happily Saunio saw what was in the wind and, although his unfortunate fellow artist had only been murdered a moment before, he promptly walked on to the stage and started to do a turn: "Ladies and gentlemen, here is luck! Well cut,

[1] At Asculum, a Confederate state which formed an enclave in Roman territory. The Italian Confederates of Rome had long been demanding the Roman franchise, and a civil war between Citizens and Confederates was on the point of breaking out all over Italy. [ED.]

[2] It was this which made the situation so dangerous in view of the tense state of feeling on both sides, for the rest of the audience naturally consisted of the Confederate population of Asculum itself. The two parties were thus intermingled at close quarters, and a single spark might produce an explosion. [ED.]

[3] *I.e.*, by the Confederates. [ED.]

[4] *I.e.*, the highest class of Confederate status, which carried with it some of the privileges of citizenship. [ED.]

Sir! All is well that begins badly, I hope. You know, I am not a Roman, but one of yourselves. I travel all round Italy, but I never see the last of Roman pussy with her nine tails. What do I travel in? My own humble gifts. And what am I after? A good time for you. That is what I call salesmanship. You wouldn't hurt the world's little swallow? I nest in all your houses and nobody minds me. That is my privilege. Kindly pass over the bird of passage. Supposing you didn't, I am sorry to think how sorry you would be"—and so on and so forth, keeping them amused and in fits of laughter with the running fire of his patter, until he had coaxed them out of their ugly temper by his irresistible charm and felt himself out of danger.

FRATERNIZATION
(90 B.C.)
(DIODORUS: Book XXXVII, fragment 15)

MARIUS led his forces into the lowlands of Samnium and took up a position opposite the enemy,[1] whereupon Pompaedius,[2] who had been invested with the supreme command on the Marsian[3] side, ordered his own forces to advance. The armies were almost in contact when the grim spirit of war resolved itself abruptly into a pacific disposition. As soon as the troops on either side had approached close enough for mutual recognition, they found themselves recognizing numbers of personal friends, renewing acquaintance with not a few former comrades in arms, and identifying quantities of connections and relatives.[4] The force of sympathy drew ejaculations of friendship from their lips. They started to hail one another by name with entreaties to refrain from the crime of slaughtering their kin. The weapons leveled in battle order were thrown aside and right hands were stretched out to greet one another in friendly salutation.

As soon as Marius noticed what was happening, he ad-

[1] The Italian Confederates of Rome, a number of whom had seceded owing to their failure, after long efforts, to obtain the Roman franchise by constitutional methods. The civil war between Citizens and Confederates became involved with the party struggles within the Roman citizen body itself, and was not completely terminated until 81 B.C. [ED.]

[2] Quintus Pompaedius Silo, a citizen of the Confederate Canton Marsica, who had taken a leading part in the constitutional struggle for the franchise before the military struggle began. [ED.]

[3] The Marsians had taken the lead among the insurgent Confederates. [ED.]

[4] The two parties were linked with one another by bonds of this character owing to the liberty of intermarriage allowed to Roman citizens and Confederates by law. [AUTHOR.]

vanced in person from the ranks; Pompaedius did the like; and the two commanders addressed one another like kinsmen. They entered into a long conversation on the subject of peace and of the coveted franchise; both armies were filled with joy and with fair hopes for a settlement; and the whole concourse relapsed from the discipline of war into an atmosphere of festivity, so that when the commanders had made overtures for peace in their personal conversation, the rank and file were delighted to be released from the duty of slaughtering one another.

IN THE THEATER AT EPHESUS
(*ca.* A.D. 57)

(*The Acts of the Apostles:* Chapter XIX, verses 23–41)

ABOUT this time *The Path* [1] became the occasion of a serious disturbance. A jeweler named Demetrius, who provided employment on a considerable scale for the members of his profession by making [souvenir] shrines of Artemis, called a meeting of his associates and of the whole trade, and addressed them as follows: "Gentlemen, you know that this employment is the source of our prosperity, and you also know, on the evidence of your eyes and ears, that in Ephesus—and not only in Ephesus but almost everywhere throughout the Province [2]—this man Paul has perverted crowds of people by saying that 'Manufactured Gods are no Gods.' The danger is not merely that this branch of our business may become discredited, but that the shrine of the Great Goddess Artemis may fall into contempt and that sooner or later she may be pulled down from her seat—she whose majesty all the province and all the world adores." Demetrius's language filled his hearers with such passion that they began to shriek the words: "Artemis of Ephesus forever!" The confusion spread till it filled the city, and the population rushed by a common impulse into the theater, after seizing Gaius and Aristarchus [3] on the way. Paul wished to face the Assembly, but he was prevented by his converts, while several members of the *Provincial Board,* [4] who were friendly to him, also sent messages

[1] One of the names by which the Christian persuasion was familiarly known among its own members. [ED.]

[2] The Roman Province of "Asia," corresponding to the modern Ottoman vilayet of Aidin in Western Anatolia. [ED.]

[3] Macedonian traveling companions of Paul. [AUTHOR.]

[4] A board of local notables, elected by the principal municipalities in the province, whose duty it was to organize (and pay for) the celebration of public festivals —the policy of the Roman Government being to provide an outlet for local ambition and to foster a sense of provincial solidarity and corporate life. [ED.]

begging him not to expose himself in the theater. Meanwhile, everybody was shrieking something different from everybody else, the meeting being in utter confusion and the majority having no notion why they had assembled. Out of the crowd they put up Alexander, who had been put forward by the Jews, and Alexander made a signal with his hand for silence with the intention of offering a public explanation. No sooner, however, had they detected that he was a Jew than the same cry issued from every throat and continued for as long as two hours: "Artemis of Ephesus forever!" Tranquillity was at last restored by the Recorder, who addressed the crowd as follows: "Gentlemen, the whole world knows that our City of Ephesus is the shrine keeper of Artemis the Great and of the Image that came down from Heaven. The facts are indisputable and, that being so, it is your duty to preserve tranquillity and to do nothing rash. These gentlemen whom you have brought here have committed neither sacrilege nor blasphemy against our Goddess. If Demetrius and his professional associates have any complaint against anybody, there are Sessions and there are Governors General—let them sue one another. If there is any point on which you still desire to be satisfied, it shall be disposed of at the Stated Meeting. Please realize that we are quite likely to be reprimanded for riot on account of this day's work, as no charge can be brought home to any individual, and that we shall have no satisfactory defense to offer in regard to it—in regard, I mean, to this concourse." With these words the Recorder dismissed the meeting.

SECTION II—CONFLICTS OF WILL

ARISTAGORAS, CLEOMENES I, AND GORGO

(ca. 499–498 B.C.)

(HERODOTUS: Book V, chapters 49–51)

ARISTAGORAS, the despot of Miletus, came to Sparta [1] while Cleomenes [2] was on the throne. According to the Lacedae-

[1] At the close of the preceding summer (probably the summer of 499 B.C.), Aristagoras had persuaded his own state of Miletus and many of the other autonomous Hellenic city-states along the west coast of Anatolia, and on the adjoining islands, to revolt against the Persian Empire. [ED.]

[2] Cleomenes I, of the Agiad Dynasty, reigned ca. 520-488 B.C. [ED.]

monian account, Aristagoras went to interview the King armed with a bronze plaque, upon which was engraved a map of the entire land and sea surface of the earth with all the rivers. He opened the conversation by addressing the King to the following effect: "King Cleomenes, you must not be surprised at my importunity in paying this visit to Sparta. The situation is this. It is a shame and a grief that the sons of Ionia should be slaves instead of free men, and while this affects us Ionians most of all, it likewise affects you Lacedaemonians more than other Hellenes, in as much as you are the leaders of the Hellenic world. So now we beg you, in the name of the Hellenic gods, to rescue the Ionians from slavery. Blood is thicker than water, and the enterprise can be carried through without causing you trouble. The Orientals are not good fighters, whereas you are a nation of soldiers who have attained the highest pinnacle of valor. Then, the Orientals' weapons are simply bows and a short spear, and they go into action equipped in trousers and caps.[1] You can see that they are no trouble to conquer. Moreover, the wealth possessed by the inhabitants of their continent is equal to that of all the rest of mankind put together. Besides gold (to begin with), there are silver and bronze and embroidered clothing and livestock—animal and human—all of which may be yours if you set your hearts upon it.

"The Asiatic populations adjoin one another in the geographical order which I shall explain to you. Next to the Ionians (here) come the Lydians (here), who occupy a fertile country and are exceedingly rich in silver.[2] Next to the Lydians" (Aristagoras continued) "come these Phrygians (here) to the east, who possess more cattle and produce more cereals than any other nation that I know. Next to the Phrygians come the Cappadocians, whom we Hellenes call 'Syrians.'[3] The Cappadocians have a common frontier with the Cilicians, who stretch down to the sea (here) in which lies (here) the Island of Cyprus. The annual tribute paid by the Cilicians to the Great King is 500 talents. Next to the Cilicians (here) come the Armenians (here), and next to the Armenians the Matieni, in this territory (here).[4] Next to the Matieni comes

[1] Whereas the Hellenic heavy infantry of the period were equipped in bronze helmets and greaves. [ED.]
[2] Aristagoras was pointing, as he spoke, to the map engraved on the plaque which he carried with him. [AUTHOR.]
[3] Probably a reminiscence of an actual Assyrian colonization of east-central and northeastern Anatolia, as early as the last quarter of the third millennium B.C., of which remains have been found by modern Western archaeologists. See *Anatolian Studies presented to Sir W. M. Ramsay* (Manchester, 1923, University Press). [ED.]
[4] The territory of the Matieni (who were grouped with the Alarodii or people of Ararat to form a single Persian province) corresponded to the Ottoman vilayets of Mosul and Van or (in more general terms) to Kurdistan. [ED.]

the country of Cissia[1] (here), in which—at last—on the banks of the River Choaspes (here) lies this city of Susa, where the Great King resides, and this is where he keeps his treasure. Take this city and, as far as wealth goes, you may cheerfully challenge comparison with Zeus himself.[2] As it is, you have to hazard battles against the Messenians (who are a match for you) and the Arcadians and the Argives, who are innocent of any relations with gold or silver—the prizes which really do inspire a man to lose his life in war—and this for territory which is neither extensive nor so very rich, but lies within narrow boundaries. Considering this, will you refuse the opportunity, now that it is offered to you, of ruling all Asia without trouble?"

When Aristagoras had finished, Cleomenes simply replied: "If you please, I will postpone my answer till the day after tomorrow," and that was as far as they went at their first interview; but, when the day fixed for the answer arrived, they kept their appointment, and then Cleomenes asked Aristagoras how many days' journey it was from the coast of Ionia to the Court of the Great King. Aristagoras was normally clever and he had been hoaxing Cleomenes superbly hitherto, but at this point he committed a blunder. He ought never to have told the truth if he really wanted to entice the Spartans into Asia, but (however it happened) he told it and mentioned the fact that it was three months' journey into the interior. Cleomenes promptly cut short the rest of the speech on the subject of the route which was on the tip of Aristagoras's tongue. "Sir," he said, "I must request you to leave Sparta before sunset. You have nothing to say which will appeal to the Lacedaemonians if you desire to take them three months' journey from the coast." With these words Cleomenes went home; but Aristagoras took an olive branch,[3] followed Cleomenes to his house, used a suppliant's privilege to enter, and adjured Cleomenes to send away the child and to give him a hearing. The child in question was Cleomenes's daughter Gorgo, who was standing beside him,[4] but Cleomenes told him to say what he wished without hesitating on the child's account. Then, at last, Aristagoras began promising him from ten talents upward, if only he would perform

---

[1] The modern Province of Ahwaz, corresponding to the ancient Elam—the lowlands of which were sometimes called Susiana, after the capital city. [Ed.]

[2] Since the family failing of the Hellenic gods was Envy, it was usually fatal for human beings to challenge comparison with them on any point—creditable or discreditable. [Ed.]

[3] An olive branch (sometimes festooned with skeins of wool) was a symbol of supplication, and placed the party to whom it was presented under an indefinite but often potent religious obligation to hear the suppliant's petition. [Ed.]

[4] She was in fact the only child he had. She was eight or nine years old. [Author.]

what he asked of him. When Cleomenes shook his head,[1] Aristagoras went on raising his figure higher and higher until he had offered the sum of fifty talents—at which point the child broke out: "Father, the stranger will corrupt you if you do not leave him and go away." Thereupon Cleomenes, delighted at the child's advice, proceeded to leave the room, while Aristagoras left Sparta altogether, without succeeding in explaining any further details of the journey inland to the Court of the Great King.

THE WAR DEBATE AT SPARTA
(432 B.C.)
(THUCYDIDES: Book I, chapters 67–88, and Book II, chapter 12)

THE Lacedaemonians called a general conference of their Allies and other parties who had complaints against the Athenians, and requested them to state their case before a regular meeting of the Spartan Assembly. At this meeting the speakers successively unfolded their grievances. The Megarians had many differences with Athens to detail, the most serious being their exclusion, contrary to treaty, from all harbors in the Athenian Empire and from the home market of Attica. The last to rise were the Corinthians, who waited until their colleagues had worked upon the feelings of the Lacedaemonians before delivering their stroke. The sense of their speech was as follows:

"Lacedaemonians! Your confidence in your own constitution and in your own public life inclines you to be skeptical toward representations from foreigners. This may fortify your judgment, but it undoubtedly puts you out of touch with foreign affairs. When we have warned you, as we have often done, of the injuries threatening us from the Athenians, you have generally omitted to inform yourselves of the facts laid before you and have preferred to suspect us of being inspired by private interests. That is why you have not called the Allies together here until the blow has fallen and the crisis is upon us. Of all the Allies, we have the best title to speak, since we have the most serious complaints to bring. Our honor is being insulted by the Athenians, our interests neglected by you.

---

[1] Literally, "raised his head." The Hellenes (like the modern Greeks) nodded, in our Western way, as a sign of the affirmative, but raised the head (and no doubt half-closed the eyes and drew down the corners of the mouth simultaneously, as the modern Greeks do) to indicate denial or refusal. [ED.]

"Had they been injuring Hellas unobtrusively, it might have been part of our duty to enlighten you regarding the facts; but the Athenians have spared us that trouble by trampling, before your eyes, upon the liberties of some countries, by plotting against others, including our Allies, and by their long-perfected preparedness for the eventuality of war. What do they mean by surreptitiously accepting the advances of Corcyra in order to hold the island against us by force, or by besieging Potidaea? Potidaea is a first-rate base for operations on the Thracian Littoral. Corcyra would have contributed an important naval contingent to our Confederacy.

"For all this you are responsible. In the first place you allowed the Athenians to fortify their town after the Persian War, and later to erect the Long Walls, and from then till now you have been cheating of their liberty not only the countries enslaved by Athens but latterly your own Allies. The ultimate responsibility attaches not to the power committing the crime against liberty but to the power permitting it when in a position to interfere, however much that power may have made its reputation as the liberator of Hellas. It has not been easy to secure our present meeting and even now we are not facing the facts. The time has gone by for discussing whether we are suffering injuries; and while we do not know our own minds, the aggressors have made up theirs and are losing no time. We are familiar with Athenian methods. Making their encroachments on their neighbors step by step, as they do, they have still some misgivings so long as they believe that they are simply profiting by your insensitiveness; but when once they realize that your inactivity is not for want of knowledge, they will throw all their strength into their attack. You Lacedaemonians are the only people in Hellas who quietly wait and see, instead of meeting force with force. You are the only people who delay until your enemy has doubled his strength before you destroy him, instead of nipping his development in the bud. It used to be said that you could be depended upon, but you have hardly deserved that reputation. We know ourselves that the Persians were able to march from the ends of the earth to the gates of the Peloponnese before you seriously disputed their passage; and now, when the enemy is Athens— not a remote power like Persia, but our neighbor—you leave the Athenians the initiative. Instead of taking the offensive, you prefer to receive their attack and to be driven to fight with your backs to the wall through having permitted them so vastly to develop their strength. Yet you are aware that the Oriental was chiefly responsible for his own disasters, and that if we have survived our encounters with the Athenians, that too has generally been thanks to their mistakes and not to your support. Indeed, misplaced reliance upon you has already been the ruin of more than one of your friends, whose trust betrayed them into unpreparedness.

"We hope that you will not misunderstand our motives in telling you these home truths, which we do in a spirit of remonstrance and not of hostility. Pointing out the mistakes of friends is not the same thing as denouncing the crimes of enemies, and, apart from that, we consider that nobody has as good a right as we to criticize their neighbors, particularly when so profound a contrast of national temperament is involved. Have you ever realized that contrast? Have you ever thought out what your future opponents, the Athenians, are like, or how vastly, and indeed utterly, they differ from yourselves? They are revolutionaries, equally prompt in conception and execution. You are conservatives who deprecate new ideas and who take even less than the essential minimum of action. Again, they venture beyond their strength and take risks beyond their judgment, yet never lose heart in a crisis, while your temptation is to keep too far within your margin, to distrust your judgment even where there is no room for doubt, and to imagine in every crisis that all is lost. They are men of action, while you are never able to make up your minds. They travel to the ends of the earth, while you stay at home. They expect to increase their substance by going abroad, while you expect to ruin what you have in hand by going forward. They exploit their victories to the utmost and yield as little ground as possible in defeat. They place their bodies at the absolute disposal of their country, but retain the absolute disposal of their minds for forwarding that country's interests. Unattempted objectives appear to them like positions lost, while objectives won seem no more than first steps in advance. When they try and fail, they make good their loss with alternative projects. They are the only people of whom it is true that 'to hope is to have,' so instantaneously do they translate counsel into action. They pursue these ideals through toil and danger all the days of their life; perpetual acquisitiveness leaves them no leisure to enjoy what they have acquired; the only holiday they appreciate is to be about their business; and they have as much horror of unemployment as of overwork. In one word, it might truly be said that they are born never to rest themselves and never to allow rest to others.

"Those are your competitors, gentlemen, and yet you hesitate, as though the best insurance for peace were not an unmistakable determination not to tolerate injuries (always balanced by a proper use of power). Your idea is to give and take, to live and let live—an almost impossible policy even if your neighbors were as peculiar as yourselves, and an anachronism, as we have tried to demonstrate, when you have to deal with the Athenians. The triumph of progress is the law of life, as well as of economics. Rigid conservatism may be the ideal for fair weather, but emergencies require invention, and that is why the Athenians, profiting by their vast experience, have improved themselves out of all comparison with you. The time has come for you to pull yourselves together and to save the Potidaeans and their fellow victims, as you have promised, by an immediate invasion of Attica, if you do not wish to betray your friends and kinsmen to your deadliest enemies and to drive the rest of us, in despair, to look for other allies—a step which would be absolutely justified by all laws human and divine. The treaty breakers are not those who are forced by desertion to look for new friends, but those who do not honor their bond to furnish their support. Still, if you only display some energy, you need not fear that we shall leave you, for it is a strong measure to change sides and we should not easily find such sympathetic partners again. God guide your decision and grant that this great Confederacy, to the leadership of which you have been born, may not be diminished under your keeping."

When the Corinthians had finished speaking, an Athenian mission, which happened to be in Lacedaemon already on other business and had been listening to the debate, felt it desirable to intervene. Their intention was not to offer any defense against the complaints of the other powers but to explain the magnitude of the issues involved and so induce them to take their time instead of coming to hasty decisions. They were also desirous of impressing the Conference with the greatness of Athens's power, by reviving the memories of the older generation and informing the younger of facts which they could not know for themselves. A speech on such lines, they thought, might incline the meeting toward peace instead of war. They therefore approached the Lacedaemonians and expressed their wish to be allowed to address the Assembly in their turn, if that were in order. On being requested to rise, they spoke approximately as follows:

"Our mission here is not to enter into a controversy with your allies, but to carry out our instructions. Since, however, our country has been subjected in our presence to somewhat lively criticism, we rise—not in order to answer the complaints of the other powers (this Assembly not being a court whose jurisdiction either party can recognize), but to save you from being persuaded by your allies into lightly taking a wrong decision on a momentous issue. We should also like to offer some remarks upon our general position, with a view to showing that we have a reasonable title to what we possess and that our country has claims to consideration.

"We shall not trouble you with ancient history, in which the evidence rests on tradition and not on the personal experience of those present; but we cannot omit the Persian War and the events of our own lifetime, even at the risk of wearying you by continually harping on the theme. Still, the labor was not endured nor the risk run for nothing, and since you shared in the material benefits at the time, we ought not altogether to be deprived of whatever benefit may accrue to us from the story; but if we repeat it, it will not be by way of appeal, but as a pertinent testimony to the character of that power with which you will have to reckon if you take a wrong decision.

"At Marathon, then, we pride ourselves on having faced the Oriental single-handed, while, in his second invasion, when we found ourselves too weak to resist him on land, we joined the navy to the last man and fought him on sea at Salamis—the battle which prevented him from sailing against the countries of the Peloponnese and destroying them piecemeal, incapable as they would have been of coming to one another's assistance when attacked by so numerous a fleet as his. The most decisive witness to our achievement is the enemy himself, for after his defeat at sea he confessed that he was no longer equal to the contest by beating a hasty retreat with the major part of his forces. These are the facts. They prove that sea power saved Hellas, and the three most important contributions to Hellenic sea power—the largest squadron, the ablest commander, and the most devoted service—were made by Athens. Our contingent of ships was just under two thirds of the total four hundred; our commander was Themistocles, to whom belongs the chief credit for having accepted battle in the Straits,[1] which admittedly saved the situation (as you yourselves confessed when you afterward received him with greater honors than any previous foreign visitor); while our service was the most gallant of any given to the cause. Nobody was supporting us on land; every Hellenic country up to our frontiers had surrendered its liberty; and yet, when we had evacuated our town and lost all that we had to lose, we refused to abandon the cause of our remaining allies, as we should have done if we had broken up and ceased to be a military factor. Instead, we manned our ships and faced death with you, without resenting your previous failure to come to our assistance. We consider, therefore, that we are at least even with you on this account. At the time when *you* helped *us*, your homes were still standing, you looked forward to their remaining

---

[1] Between the mainland of Attica and the Island of Salamis. [ED.]

yours, and your anxiety was for your own sakes rather than for ours (so long as we still had homes to save, you had failed to stand by us). At the time when *we* faced death with *you* and did our part to save you in addition to saving ourselves, our country had ceased to exist and we had the slenderest hopes of recovering it. Yet if anxiety for our homes had induced us, as it induced others, to desert to the Persians at the beginning, or had afterward robbed us, like broken men, of the spirit to man our ships, you had not enough ships of your own to contemplate a naval battle, and the enemy would have achieved his war aims without further effort.

"Surely, gentlemen, the devotion and the judgment which we displayed in the Great Persian War ought to weigh against the extreme odium with which the public opinion of Hellas regards our Empire. That empire grew out of the war, and was not acquired by violence. It was your unwillingness to carry the operations to their conclusion that brought the Allies to our door and led them to offer us the command on their own initiative; and from that moment the logic of events drove us to build up our present position, under pressure principally of fear, reinforced by pride and latterly by self-interest. Once the Empire was established, the risk involved in giving it up had become too great to run. We had incurred almost universal hatred; some of our Allies had already seceded and had been reduced by force; your old cordiality toward us had changed to hostility and suspicion; and every state that seceded from us would have rallied to you. No one can be blamed for consulting his own interests in questions of life and death. You yourselves have interfered in the internal affairs of the Peloponnesian states in order to promote your own interests and ascendency; and had it been you, and not we, that had persevered to the end of the Persian War, perpetuated your ascendency and incurred the hatred which that ascendency entailed, we feel sure that your hand would have been felt at least as heavy as ours, and that you would have been confronted with the very same dilemma of either ruling by force or jeopardizing your own existence. This should make you realize that we were not inhuman monsters if we accepted an empire when it was offered to us and then succumbed to the three strongest human motives—pride, fear, and interest—in refusing to give it up. Nor are we the first to sin. The dominion of the strong over the weak is the law of History; and, besides, we felt ourselves and were felt by you to deserve the position—that is, until self-interest inspired you with your present devotion to 'International Right,' which has never yet deterred a human being from exploiting his advantage whenever there has been anything to be gained by force. Some credit, however, may possibly be due to those who pay more respect to 'Right' than their power necessitates after they have successfully followed the natural human instinct to establish their dominion over others. We venture to think that little further proof would be needed of our own moderation if once our Empire were to pass into other hands.

"Even our good nature has, most unfairly, been turned to our discredit. After putting ourselves at a disadvantage to the nationals of Allied States in mixed commercial litigation, and placing our own courts at their disposal as impartial tribunals, we have gained nothing but a reputation for litigiosity. Yet none of the malcontents has stopped to consider why this reproach is not leveled at other imperial powers who show less consideration toward their subjects, the truth being that those who are in a position to use force are under no compulsion to go to law. Our own subjects, however, have been so much spoilt by being treated on equal terms that if ever they are put at a disadvantage, either by judgment of court or by the exercise of our imperial power, and happen to consider that justice has miscarried, they are not in the least degree thankful for escaping so lightly, but take their grievance more to heart than if we had put justice on one side from the beginning and had cynically exploited our position. Had we done so, they themselves would not have ventured to dispute the principle that the weak must give way to the strong; but apparently injustice arouses greater resentment than *force majeure*, exploitation by an equal being more humiliating than compulsion from a master. After submitting to far more atrocious treatment from the Persians as a matter of course, they feel our Empire intolerable. There is nothing strange in that, for subject peoples vent their discontent upon the rulers of the day; and if you were to depose us and to rule in our stead, you would soon lose the popularity that you have reaped from the fear inspired by us, especially if your record during your brief period of command against the Persians is any indication of how you would behave today. Your rules of conduct are incompatible with any others, and, besides, the Spartan abroad neither carries his own rules with him nor adopts the general practice of civilized Hellas.

"Do not be hasty in taking such a momentous decision. Do not bring trouble upon yourselves in deference to others' opinions and others' complaints. Consider seriously the immense uncertainty of war before you find yourselves involved in it. The longer it lasts the more it reduces itself to a matter of chance, which is equally beyond the control and the prevision of both the belligerents whose fate hangs upon the issue. In going to war, nations plunge first into action, which ought to be the second stage, and do not begin to use their reason until they find themselves in trouble. At present, neither we nor you (so far as we can see) show any symptoms of this aberration. We implore you, while it still lies in the hands of both of us to take the right decision, not to dishonor your signature by breaking the treaty, but to refer our difference to arbitration as the agreement provides. If you refuse, we shall know how to defend ourselves against every form of aggression in a war not brought about by us, and may the gods defend the right."

With the conclusion of the Athenians' speech, the Lacedae-monians had heard both the complaints of their Allies against Athens and a statement from the Athenian side, and they proceeded to withdraw into private session. The majority were approaching a consensus that the Athenians had now definitely put themselves in the wrong and that war should be declared forthwith, when King Archidāmus, whose ability and judgment were rated equally high, rose and addressed them as follows:

"Gentlemen, I have fought in many wars myself, and so have my contemporaries whom I see among you today. To old soldiers, war offers neither the attraction of the unknown, as possibly it may do to the majority, nor the illusion of merits either positive or negative; and if you examine in cold blood the war which is now under your consideration, you will find yourselves faced with one of no small dimensions. This will not be a war against our neighbors in the Peloponnese, where we are confronted by powers of our own class and can strike straight at our objectives. It will be a war against an enemy whose territory is out of range and who leads the world in naval technique and in armaments (in which I include wealth, both private and public, as well as ships, mounts, munitions, and man power, in the last of which they are stronger than any other single country in Hellas); in addition to all of which, they possess a large number of tributary allies. What facilities have we for making war on a power of this character? And what are our assets if we plunge into war unprepared? Sea power? We are inferior on the sea, and training and counter-preparations involve the element of time. Money power, per-haps? But our inferiority in this field is even more decisive. Our treasuries are empty and we are not good taxpayers. Pos-sibly we might rely on the superior strength and valor of our land forces, which could overrun and devastate their territory. But they have other territory in abundance in their Empire, and can import what they need from overseas. We might, of course, attempt to liberate their Allies, but that strategy, to be effective, requires sea power again, for these Allies are mostly islanders. How are we to wage such a war? If we fail to deprive the enemy of their command of the sea and of the revenues by which their navy is maintained, we shall suffer more damage than we can inflict; and then we shall no longer be able to secure peace with honor, especially if we appear in the light of aggressors. It would be folly to delude ourselves with the hope that the war will soon be over if we devastate their territory. On the contrary, I fear that we may bequeath this war to our children. The Athenians are a spirited people. They will certainly not be the slaves of their territory nor lose their morale as if the realities of war were new to them.

"Do not misunderstand me. I am not suggesting that we should be insensitive or that we should permit them to injure our Allies without unmasking their designs. I merely deprecate an immediate resort to arms, and propose as an alternative that we should send them a protest couched in ambiguous terms and should make use of the delay for preparations on our side. We must recruit allies both in Hellas and outside it, with a special view to the reinforcement of our sea power and our money power. In a struggle for existence there is nothing invidious in joining forces with any power in the world, whether civilized or not, which finds itself exposed, like us, to the Athenian menace. At the same time, we must mobilize our own resources. If they pay some attention to our representations, that will be the best solution. In the opposite event, we shall be better equipped for attacking them (supposing that we still desire to do so) if we delay for two or three years. Possibly, when they observe our military preparations and the corresponding tone of our diplomacy, they will be more inclined to give way while their territory remains undevastated and their property, instead of being already ruined, still exists to be a factor in their decision. Their territory is nothing less than a hostage in our hands, and a better hostage the more highly developed it is, so that it is advisable to respect it as long as possible and not to make them more intransigent by reducing them to despair. If we allow ourselves to be carried away by the complaints of our Allies and devastate Attica without being otherwise prepared for war, we may be in danger of compromising both the honor and the interests of the Peloponnese. Complaints are capable of settlement, whether countries or individuals are concerned; but if we embark upon a general war on behalf of private interests—a war the course of which it is impossible to foresee—it will not be easy to find a solution that will save our faces.

"There would be nothing cowardly in hesitating to attack Athens because she is a single power and we are many. That is a fallacious view, for she is our equal even in numbers if you count her tributary Allies, and the sinews of war are not armaments but money, which endows armaments with their efficacy—particularly in wars between land powers and sea powers. Our first business is to raise money before we allow ourselves to be moved by our Allies. On our shoulders will fall the chief responsibility for success or failure; on us, therefore, it is especially incumbent to take our time and to look ahead. Our slowness and hesitation, which are the principal targets of their criticism, are nothing to be ashamed of. 'More haste, less speed,' where haste means beginning when imperfectly prepared. At any rate, we have never failed to keep our country free or to make her famous, and the very qualities that they criticize may prove to be simply judgment and self-control. Whatever they are, they preserve us, alone in Hellas, from being thrown off our balance by success or being demoralized by failure. We are affected neither by flattery nor by abuse, and it is no more possible to push us into adventures against our judgment by the one method than it is by the other. If we are good soldiers and good statesmen, we have to thank our discipline. We are soldierly because of the intimate connection between self-control and self-respect and between self-respect and courage; while we are statesmanlike because we are not educated to be so clever as to despise the rules of the game, but with a sternness which inspires us with sufficient self-control to observe them. Our abilities are not wasted on such useless accomplishments as brilliant theoretical criticisms of the enemy's armaments followed by fiascos at the front. We are taught to think that our neighbors' minds work in much the same way as our own, and that the Fortune of War cannot be analyzed by logic. We are careful to assume that our enemies are no fools, and to take corresponding precautions, for good soldiers never depend upon the enemy's possible mistakes, but upon their own care and foresight. The truth is that the intrinsic differences between individuals are negligible, and that the victory is to those who are trained in the strictest essentials.

"This is the tradition which we have inherited from our fathers and which we have never had reason to regret ourselves. We must not betray it by allowing ourselves to be rushed. We must not take, in a fraction of a single day, decisions involving many lives, fortunes, countries, and reputations. We must take our time, and we have a sufficient margin of strength to be able to afford it. I move, therefore, that we lodge a protest at Athens with reference to Potidaea, and another with reference to the alleged injuries to our Allies. It must not be forgotten that the Athenians are willing to submit to arbitration, and it is contrary to International Law to seek satisfaction by arms so long as arbitration is offered. At the same time, I move that we prepare simultaneously for war.

This is the best decision for ourselves and the most formidable for our enemies."

As soon as Archidamus had finished, Sthenelaïdas, a member of the Directory[1] for the year, rose and terminated the debate with a speech to the following effect:—

"The long speech which we have heard from the Athenians has left me none the wiser. They found plenty to say in praise of themselves, but they never met the charge that they were inflicting injuries upon our Allies and upon the Peloponnese. If they once behaved well against the Persians before they started to behave badly toward us, they deserve a double chastisement for having changed for the worse. There has been no change in us, and, if we are well advised, we shall not look on while our Allies are being injured, and shall not postpone our intervention, considering that the Allies have not succeeded in postponing their sufferings. Other countries may have funds and ships and mounts, but we have good Allies, who must not be betrayed to the Athenians, nor left to settle their case by words (which is what they mean by arbitration) when they are suffering not in word but in act and deed. No! We must intervene forthwith and that with all our might. Let no one tell me that it is our business to reflect when injuries are being done to us. If it is for anybody to reflect and to take his time, it is for the aggressor. Gentlemen, show yourselves worthy of Sparta by voting for war. Stop the aggrandizement of the Athenians; shrink from the betrayal of our Allies; forward against the aggressor, with the gods behind us!"

In his capacity of Director he proceeded to put the question to the vote. In the Spartan Assembly they ordinarily tell by acclamation and not by ballot, but Sthenelaïdas professed inability to distinguish which shout was the louder, because he wished to stimulate their will to war by making them openly declare their decision. Accordingly, he designated a particular spot and requested all members who voted that peace had been broken by an infringement of the treaty on the Athenian side to divide in that direction, and members voting the contrary in the other. When they divided, those who voted that the treaty had been broken found themselves in an overwhelming majority. Thereupon they summoned their Allies and informed them that they had decided, for their part, that the Athenians had infringed the treaty, but that they desired to take a vote of the Allies in full conference, in order that, if war were declared, it might be in pursuance of a joint decision. After securing this result, the delegates of the Allies returned home,

---

[1] Sparta was a constitutional monarchy in which an annually elected board of five "Directors" exercised (except with armies in the field) the real executive power. [ED.]

and the Athenian mission left later, after carrying out its original instructions. The decision, in which the Spartan Assembly voted that peace had been broken, was taken when the Thirty Years' Peace, concluded after the campaign in Euboea,[1] had still sixteen years to run. The determining factor in the minds of the Lacedaemonians when they voted that peace had been broken and that there was no alternative to war, was not the impression produced by the case of their Allies, but the fear that Athens, whom they already saw mistress of the greater part of Hellas, might increase her power still further.

. . . .

Before passing the frontier,[2] Archidamus dispatched to Athens the Spartiate Melēsippus, son of Diacritus, on the chance that the Athenians might be more inclined to give way now that they saw the enemy actually on the march. The Athenians, however, would neither receive the envoy within their walls nor give him an audience in the Assembly, where Pericles's motion that no *parlementaire* or mission should be received when once the Lacedaemonians had mobilized had already secured a majority. They sent him back without listening to him, with a warning to be across the frontier within twenty-four hours and to advise his Government to hold back any further missions which they might desire to send until their troops had retired into their home territories. An escort was sent with Melesippus to prevent him from communicating with any persons on the way; they reached the frontier line; and his parting words were: "This day will be the beginning of great evils for Hellas." When he arrived at the Peloponnesian camp and Archidamus realized that the Athenians were not yet in a mood for giving way, he set his forces in motion and advanced into Athenian territory.

ATHENS AND MITYLENE
(427 B.C.)
(THUCYDIDES: Book III, chapters 35–50)

ON his arrival at Mitylēnē, Paches[3] reduced the towns of Pyrrha and Eresus, discovered the Lacedaemonian representative Salaethus in hiding in Mitylene itself, and sent him to

[1] In 446 B.C. [ED.]
[2] In the spring of 431. [ED.]
[3] The Athenian commander who had just succeeded in quelling a dangerous revolt of the State of Mitylene on the Island of Lesbos, which was one of the most powerful and most privileged of Athens's allies. [ED.]

Athens with the Mitylenaeans whom he had interned in Tenedos and with other persons whom he considered responsible for the revolt. He also sent home the greater part of his forces, but remained in Lesbos with the rest in order to impose a settlement on Mitylene and the other states of the island.

When Salaethus and the prisoners arrived, the Athenians at once put Salaethus to death, though he guaranteed, among other things, to raise the siege of Plataea, which was still being blockaded by the Peloponnesians. The fate of the other prisoners was debated in the Assembly, and in the heat of the moment it was resolved to put to death not merely those deported to Athens but all male Mitylenaeans of military age, and to sell the women and children into slavery. It told heavily against the people of Mitylene that they had revolted at all, considering that they had never been deprived of their liberty like the other Allies; and the vindictiveness of the Athenians was accentuated by the fact that the relief of Mitylene had been the objective of the Peloponnesian squadron in its adventurous raid to Ionia, from which they inferred that the revolt had been long prepared. Accordingly, they dispatched a warship to Paches to inform him of the resolutions, with orders to be prompt in putting them into effect. Next day, however, there was a reaction, since it did not take them long to realize the atrocious enormity of their decision to exterminate an entire community instead of confining themselves to the punishment of the guilty. The Mitylenaean representatives at Athens and their Athenian supporters perceived the change of feeling and induced the Government to reopen the debate. The Government, on their side, were not unwilling, since it was equally evident to them that the majority of the Assembly desired an opportunity for further discussion. The Assembly met forthwith, and a debate ensued, in the course of which the following speech was delivered by Cleon, son of Cleaenetus, who had carried the motion for the death penalty on the previous day:[1]

"It has often been borne in upon me that a democracy is incapable of governing an empire, but never so emphatically as by your present change of mind in the case of the Mitylenaeans. Your habitual security from intrigue and danger at home determines your attitude toward the Allies, and you allow them to confuse your judgment or to work upon your feelings without realizing that this amiable weakness toward them is endangering your existence through the blunders into which it leads you. Are you blind to the fact that your Empire

[1] He was the most violent man at Athens and also by far the most influential politician at the time. [AUTHOR.]

is a despotism which your subjects loathe to endure and plot to overthrow? Or that they do not obey you out of gratitude for the indulgence with which you treat them at your own expense, but out of respect for your superior strength, which has nothing to do with their feelings? But the most serious disaster will be if no motion carried in this Assembly is to stand secure, and if we fail to realize that bad legislation upheld is better for a country than good legislation of no validity. Ignorance and self-control make a better combination than cleverness and indiscipline, and the plain man is generally a better citizen of his country than the genius. Your genius is anxious to show himself wiser than the laws of the land and to play the devil's advocate in politics as the finest possible field for the advertisement of his abilities, and that is why he so often brings his country to ruin. Your plain man, on the other hand, distrusts his own intelligence and resigns himself to being less clever than the laws and incompetent to criticize a statesmanlike proposition when he hears it—an attitude which makes him an impartial judge instead of a competitor in the arena, or makes him, in other words, a successful politician. We public men should follow the plain man's example and should not be tempted by cleverness and the wish to shine into giving the country advice which is contrary to our honest opinions.

"On the question before us, my own opinion has not changed, and I am equally amazed at the conduct of the Government and at the psychology of my opponents. By reopening the debate, the Government have introduced a delay which benefits nobody but the guilty parties, for time dulls the victim's resentment against the criminal, while the more closely punishment follows at the heels of the crime the more effective is the retaliation. As regards my opponents, I shall be interested to see who will attempt to answer me by demonstrating that the offenses of the Mitylenaeans against us are to our advantage or conversely that our misfortunes are anything but an advantage to our Allies. Either he must have sufficient confidence in his abilities as a speaker to argue that an unquestionable decision of this Assembly has not been carried, or else it has been made worth his while to attempt to mislead you by some *tour de force* of advocacy. In such competitions the country gives away the prizes and shoulders the risks in exchange, and the responsibility is yours for the preposterous rules under which you play the game. You use your eyes for debate and your ears for action; in looking forward to the future you take a clever speaker's word at its face value, and in looking back at the past you close your eyes to the evidence and open your ears to specious criticism. You are the easiest prey to any new idea and the most obstinate rebels against established truths; you are slaves to the latest novelty who consider anything familiar beneath your notice. The supreme ambition of each one of you is to be a speaker himself, and, short of that, to hold your own against your heroes by never letting yourselves appear to lag behind their thought, by applauding each point before it is made, and by being as sharp-witted in anticipating a line of argument as you are slow in foreseeing its inevitable chain of effects. In fact, you have started in quest of an imaginary world before you have properly grasped the world in which we live. You are as utterly incapable of resisting the pleasures of the ear as if you were sitting at the feet of some 'uplifter' in a lecture room instead of debating public business in this Assembly.

"I must attempt to lead you into better ways by demonstrating that Mitylene has done you greater injury than any other single country. Personally, I can make some allowance for a rebel who has found our Empire intolerable or has acted under pressure from the enemy. But what of rebels who live on a fortified island, who have no attack to fear from the enemy except by sea, an element on which, so far from being defenseless, they possess naval forces of their own, and who are in enjoyment of autonomy and of a privileged relationship with you? That is not mere rebellion (which presupposes ill-usage) but a treacherous stab in the back, an attempt to join hands with our most implacable enemies for our undoing, a more deadly offense than any independent challenge to our power. They took no warning from the disasters of their neighbors whose revolts against us had been crushed before. They were not restrained by their present prosperity from putting their fortunes to the touch. They went to war with a blind confidence in the future, with hopes that outshot their strength but fell far short of their ambitions, and with a cynicism that did not scruple to place might before right and to deliver an unprovoked attack upon us the moment that they felt certain of success. The truth is that nothing turns a nation's head so fatally as sudden and unexpected prosperity. Success which has some rational basis is generally less dangerous to mankind than the gifts of Fortune, and it is really easier to repel adversity than to preserve felicity. The application of the moral to the Mitylenaeans is that they ought never to have been singled out by you for differential treatment, in which case they would have been saved from this fearful fall. Contempt for deference and respect for firmness are fundamental traits of human nature; but it is not too late for the Mitylenaeans to receive the punishment that they deserve, and the upper class must not be made the scapegoats for the mass of the people. They were all of one mind in attacking you, though, if they had sided with us, they might by this time have been restored to their country. But no, they thought that to side with their upper class was the lesser risk, and so they joined in the rebellion. You must also consider the effect upon your other Allies. If you impose no greater penalties for deliberate treason than for disloyalty under pressure from the enemy, the slenderest pretext will serve every one of them for secession. For them, the prize of success will be liberation and there will be a limited liability to the penalties of failure; while for us the stakes in every struggle with a rebel will be our lives and fortunes. If we win, we shall recover nothing but the wreck of a country and shall so be deprived ever after of the revenues which are the secret of our power. If we lose, we shall have added to the number of our adversaries, and instead of being free to defend ourselves against our existing opponents, we shall be occupied in fighting our own Allies.

"Neither casuistry nor corruption must induce you to give them one vestige of hope in the names of 'Mercy' and 'Humanity.' They were not unwilling agents but deliberate traitors, and there can be no pardon unless there was no intention of ill. Personally, therefore, I stand where I have stood from the beginning; I protest against the reversal of your previous resolution; and I implore you to beware of the three failings—pity, sentiment, and good nature—which are fatal to empire. Compassion should be shown toward those who reciprocate it, not toward those who are incapable of doing so and who are your natural and irreconcilable enemies. The speakers who charm us by their eloquence can find less dangerous fields for displaying their talent, instead of choosing an issue in which the country will pay a heavy penalty for a brief recreation, while these gentlemen themselves will receive fine acknowledgments for fine phrases. As for good nature, it is better employed in being shown toward those who will be our friends in the future, not toward our unalterable and implacable foes. In a word, if you take my advice, you will be dealing justly by the Mitylenaeans and in your own interest as well; while, if you decide otherwise, you will not be obliging them so much as passing sentence on yourselves. If they had a right to rebel, then you have no right to your Empire; and if, right or wrong, you are determined to hold it, then justice must be sacrificed to expediency and the Mitylenaeans must suffer, or else you must abdicate and cultivate your morality out of harm's way. No, make up your minds to pay them in their own coin. Because you have escaped their treachery, why show yourselves less alive to feeling than the traitors? Think what you would have had to expect from them had they been the victors, especially when the aggression was on their side. It is the unprovoked aggressors who wage the wars of extermination. They know that for them an enemy spared is a standing danger, because the survivor of a wanton assault cherishes resentment for what, in fair fight, he would have forgiven.

"Do not be traitors to yourselves. Try to feel as you felt at the moment when you received their cowardly blow. Remember the supreme importance you attached to their reduction, and requite them now that the time has come, without losing your nerve at the critical moment and without letting yourselves forget the peril that hung over you so short a while ago. Punish the Mitylenaeans as they deserve and warn the other Allies, by a signal example, that the penalty of rebellion is death. When once they realize that, you will less often be distracted from fighting the enemy by having to fight your own Allies."

When Cleon had finished speaking, he was followed by Diodotus, son of Eucrătes, who had led the opposition to the death sentence at the previous sitting. Diodotus now rose again and spoke as follows:

"I have no fault to find with the Government for reopening the debate on the Mitylenaeans, nor sympathy with members who object to the reconsideration of vital issues. In my opinion, the two insuperable obstacles to statesmanship are haste and passion—haste being the sure sign of folly and passion of vulgarity and narrowness of mind. Anyone who contends that action has nothing to learn from debate is either a fool or a knave—a fool, if he supposes it possible to deal in any other medium with the future when it still lies beyond the horizon; a knave, if the policy that he wishes to carry is so abominable that he despairs of finding good arguments for it and therefore resorts to vilification, in the hope that he may possibly prove good enough at that to frighten his opponents and his audience. It is even more intolerable to accuse a member of corrupt motives for supporting a motion. If mere ignorance were the imputation, the unsuccessful speaker might have retired with a slur upon his intelligence but not upon his honor; but when honor is impugned, success itself becomes suspicious, while failure is as fatal to the speaker's moral as it is to his intellectual reputation. This state of things is not in the interests of the country, whose natural advisers are thereby deterred from serving her. She would have everything to gain if members who behave in this way were inhibited from speaking. Their countrymen would then be misled less often than they are. A man of public spirit does not attempt to terrorize his opponents but to overcome them in fair argument; and a wise nation, short of rewarding its best advisers, refrains from penalizing them, while, so far from punishing bad statesmanship, it refuses even to disgrace its author. That is the way to prevent successful statesmen from sacrificing their convictions to popularity for the sake of higher honors, and unsuccessful statesmen from clutching at the same dishonest expedient for winning public opinion to their side.

"That, unfortunately, is not our way; and, indeed, if anyone is so much as suspected of corrupt motives for offering advice which is unimpeachable in itself, we so far give way to our feelings that on a mere suspicion against the author of the policy we deprive the country of its certain benefits. The consequence is that good advice honestly given has become just as suspect as its opposite, and that as many lies are needed to vouch for respectable policies as to deceive the people into adopting the most monstrous propositions. Our subtle Athens is the only country which it is impossible to serve straightforwardly and without disguise, since open offers of loyal service merely provoke suspicions of some hidden personal aim. And yet, in our present situation and with vital issues to be faced, we statesmen must make it our duty to look beyond your comparatively narrow range of vision, especially when we have to bear responsibility for advice given to an irresponsible audience. If carrying and adopting a policy involved equal penalties, you would be more cautious in coming to your decisions; but, as it is, you frequently allow yourselves to be misled by the passion of the moment and then penalize the single vote of the mover, while passing over your own, which were equally wrong and many times more numerous.

"My own object, in rising to speak on the question before us, is neither to offer opposition nor to make accusations; for, if we are well advised, we shall not allow the conduct of the Mitylenaeans to enter into the issue, but shall confine it to our own interests. Even if I were in a position to demonstrate that the Mitylenaeans were completely in the wrong, I should not necessarily propose the death penalty unless our interests dictated it; nor should I propose to spare them on account of extenuating circumstances if Athens were likely to suffer. In my opinion, we are discussing a precedent rather than the particular case before us, and I shall challenge my honorable friend on his own ground. The point on which he most insists is that the death penalty will be a valuable precedent for discouraging rebellion, while I insist that its effect as a precedent will be precisely the contrary. I must beg of you in advance not to reject the utility of my contention for the plausibility of his. In your present temper against Mitylene, his contention may perhaps attract you as more just; but this is a political assembly and not a court of law, and the issue before us is not what the Mitylenaeans deserve but how it best suits us to treat them.

"In all countries the death penalty is on the statute book for a number of offenses, some of which, I grant you, are considerably less heinous than that of the Mitylenaeans. Yet Hope nerves the criminal to take the risk, and I have never heard of anyone who took it in the conviction that he would not survive the attempt. Nor have I heard of a country consciously embarking on a revolt with inadequate resources (of its own or in the shape of support from abroad). In politics, as in private life, humanity is born to err, and no law in the world will prevent it, or legislators would never have gone through the whole gamut of penalties in the vain search for security against evildoers. In all probability the penalties enacted for the most serious crimes were originally less severe, and have been raised to the death penalty (as most of them have) in consequence of repeated transgressions; but the death penalty, too, is set at defiance, and the law must either discover some more effective sanction or admit that the prospect of death is no deterrent, so long as men are drawn into danger by poverty, with its necessity that knows no fear; by power, with its unbalanced pride that knows no satisfaction; or by the other situations of life with the various irresistible passions that so fatally enthrall them. All life, moreover, is dominated by the two evil geniuses of Hope and Desire—Desire that leads and Hope that follows; Desire that plots and plans and Hope that draws the draft on Fortune—two unseen powers that are mightier far than any terrors visible to the eye. Their influence is reinforced by their potent ally Fortune, who often lures her victims, by her unexpected aid, into facing fearful odds; and her greatest victims are nations, which play for the supreme stakes of liberty or empire, and in which each individual irrationally magnifies his powers as a member of the herd. No, it is inconceivable, it is nonsensical, to suppose that when human nature takes the bit between its teeth, the power of the law or any other deterrent can guide its feet out of the paths of destruction.

"We must not, therefore, allow a mistaken belief in the efficacy of the death penalty as a guarantee to lead us into a wrong decision, as it will do if we leave future rebels no hope of finding a place for repentance or for retracing their false step at the first opportunity. Remember that, up till now, rebellion has not been irrevocable and that if the rebel country realizes that its cause is hopeless, it is always prepared to come to terms while still in a condition to pay an indemnity and a permanent contribution. But if you create this precedent, there is not one prospective rebel that will not prepare more thoroughly than heretofore and hold out to the last extremity, if no better terms are to be purchased by early than by late surrender. This impossibility of coming to terms can only be to our disadvantage. A protracted siege will multiply our expenses, and, even if the operations are crowned with success, we shall 'recover nothing but the wreck of a country' and 'shall be deprived ever after of the revenues' from it 'which are the secret of our military power.' No, gentlemen, we must not prejudice our interests by exacting the strict justice of the courts from these offenders. We must see that the punishment which we inflict is sufficiently mild to conserve the money power of our subjects and to retain it at our disposal; and we must look for our guarantees not to the severity of the law but to the efficiency of our supervision. At present we do the opposite, and when free peoples, forcibly subjected to our Empire, take the perfectly natural course of rebelling in the name of independence, we feel called upon to signalize the suppression of their revolt by inflicting condign punishment. But the secret of dealing with free men is to concentrate not upon punishing rebellion when it occurs but upon preventing its occurrence by vigilance beforehand; and if you cannot close all avenues to the entrance of the idea into their minds, you can at least limit the responsibility when the incident is over.

"Here is another capital blunder into which the policy of my honorable friend would lead you. At present, the masses in all the subject states are well-disposed toward you, and either refuse altogether to join the upper classes in rebelling, or, if their hand is forced, adopt a hostile attitude toward the rebels from the outset. This secures you the support of the masses in any rebel state before you commence operations; but if you exterminate the masses at Mitylene, who have had no part or lot in this rebellion and who voluntarily surrendered the town from the moment that they had possessed themselves of arms, in the first place you will be committing a gross injustice by rewarding a service with death, and in the second place you will be playing into the hands of the ruling class. Henceforward, whenever they plunge their country into rebellion, the masses will not hesitate to take their side, for they will have had clear warning from you that the innocent and the guilty are to be punished without discrimination. It would be better, even if their guilt were proved, to ignore it, rather than to alienate the only element in the subject states that supports you. If policy is to be judged by its contribution to the maintenance of our Empire, then it is more politic to submit to injuries than to indulge our craving for justice by inopportune severity. My honorable friend has suggested that justice and interest will both be satisfied by the punishment that he proposes. My analysis proves that, on the contrary, they are incompatible.

"I ask you to decide in favor of my policy on its own merits, without being swayed by pity or good nature, the influence of which I am as anxious to eliminate as my honorable friend; and my policy is to put the prisoners deported by Paches on their trial for treason (in due course), and to leave the rest of the population of Mitylene in peace. Besides being the best policy in the long run, this will have an immediate effect upon the enemy's morale, for good statemanship is a more formidable weapon than the blind onslaughts of brute force."

When Diodotus had finished and these two directly contradictory motions were before the Assembly, there was still a violent conflict of opinion and the voting in the division was almost equal, but Diodotus's motion was carried by a narrow majority. Immediate steps were taken to dispatch a second warship with the least possible delay, for fear that the other might arrive first and the destruction of Mitylene be an accomplished fact. The first boat had twenty-four hours' start, but the Mitylenaean representatives at Athens supplied the second with wine and barley bread and promised large rewards if it won the race, which so greatly stimulated the crew that they took their meals (a ration of barley bread steeped in wine and oil) without leaving the oar, and slept and rowed in alternate watches. Fortunately, they encountered no adverse winds, and the other boat was not exerting itself to accomplish its repugnant mission. It reached Mitylene just sufficiently ahead for Paches to have read the decree of the Assembly, but, as he was on the point of putting it into execution, the heroic efforts of the second warship brought it into port and enabled it to deliver the reprieve in time. Mitylene was saved on the verge of destruction.

The prisoners deported by Paches as the persons chiefly responsible for the revolt were afterward put to death (to the number of rather more than a thousand) on Cleon's motion; the fortifications of Mitylene were demolished and her fleet confiscated. Instead of imposing a tribute on Lesbos, Athens subsequently divided the land (excluding the territory of Methymna[1]) into three thousand allotments, of which three hundred were consecrated and the remainder distributed by lot to Athenian applicants. The Lesbians arranged with the new owners to pay a rent for each allotment of two minas per annum, on condition that they should continue to cultivate

[1] The second strongest state on the Island of Lesbos, which had remained loyal to Athens out of jealousy toward Mitylene. [Ed.]

the land themselves. The continental possessions of Mitylene were also confiscated by Athens and passed under her sovereignty. These were the results of the Lesbian Revolt.

ATHENS AND MELOS
(416 B.C.)
(THUCYDIDES: Book V, chapters 84–116)

THE following summer . . . the Athenians also attacked the Island of Melos[1] with an expedition consisting of 30 Athenian, 6 Chian, and 2 Lesbian warships; 1200 infantry, 300 archers and 20 mounted archers of Athenian nationality; and about 1500 infantry furnished by the Allies and the Islanders. With this force, the Athenian commanders Cleomēdes, son of Lycomēdes, and Tīsias, son of Tīsimachus, landed on Melian territory, but, before inflicting any damage on the country, they first sent *parlementaires*. The Melian Government did not bring these emissaries before the Assembly but asked them to explain their mission to the authorities and the notables in private. To this the Athenian *parlementaires* replied: "If we are not to address the Assembly, presumably that is for fear that a consecutive speech from us might mislead the masses by seductive arguments which they might not be able to pick to pieces at a single hearing. (Pardon me! But we know that this is the meaning of our reception by this select company.) We therefore suggest to this committee a still safer course of procedure. Examine the issues point by point instead of making a set speech on your side either, and challenge, as it comes, any proposition of ours to which you take exception. Begin, if you please, by telling us whether the proposal itself is agreeable to you."

"There is no objection," the Melian commissioners replied, "to the fair offer that we should exchange, in a calm atmosphere, our respective points of view, but these military preparations, which are not merely imminent but actual, appear hardly compatible with your suggestion. In fact, we see that you have constituted yourselves your own judges in this debate; and the conclusion which presumably we have to expect is war, if we win our case in equity and for that reason refuse to give way, or otherwise slavery if we submit to you."

[1] The Melians are Lacedaemonian colonists and they had refused to accept Athenian domination as had been done by the other Islanders. At the beginning they had successfully preserved their neutrality, but eventually the persistent devastation of their territory by the Athenians had forced them into a state of open warfare. [AUTHOR.]

Athenian Spokesman: "Really, if you have come to this conference for no better purpose than to calculate hypothetical contingencies, and not with the strict object of advising your countrymen how to secure their salvation in the light of the facts which stare you in the face, we might as well break off the discussion. If your object is your salvation, we will go on."

Melian Spokesman: "For people in our terrible position, it is natural and excusable to explore every turning offered by thought, whether uttered or unspoken. Still—our object in this conference certainly is to secure our salvation, and the discussion, if you please, shall be conducted in the way that you propose."

Athenian: "Well, then—we have no intention on our side of presenting a long and correspondingly unconvincing statement adorned with fine phrases about our having the right to rule because we overthrew the Mede or about our present operations being reprisals for injuries received; and we beg you on your side not to imagine that you will move us by such arguments as that you did not take sides with the Lacedaemonians in spite of being their colonists and that you have committed no offense. Try to arrive at a practical settlement on the basis of what we each of us genuinely feel. You know as well as we do that, in the logic of human nature, Right only comes into question where there is a balance of power, while it is Might that determines what the strong extort and the weak concede."

Melian: "We have our own view of expediency—since we *must* deal in these terms now that you have brushed Right aside and have recommended the discussion of Interest. In our view expediency requires you not to destroy what is our common protection, but to allow everybody to profit by fairness and Right in their hour of danger and in controversy to enjoy the benefit of the doubt short of rigid demonstration. This is as much to your advantage as it is to ours, in as much as you are exposed to the heaviest vengeance if you fall—a vengeance that would make you an example to the World."

Athenian: "No, the end of our Empire, assuming that ended it is to be, is not a prospect that appalls us. It is not the other imperial peoples like the Lacedaemonians (though the Lacedaemonians are not our actual antagonists) who are implacable toward the vanquished, but ex-subjects—if ever the subjects succeed in attacking and conquering their rulers by their unaided efforts. You must allow us, however, to take this risk upon ourselves. We propose now to demonstrate, first, that we have come here in the interests of our Empire and, secondly, that the arguments which we shall expound are conducive to the salvation of your country. We wish to avoid trouble in imposing our Empire upon you and to consult our mutual interests by saving you from destruction."

Melian: "It may be in your interest to impose your Empire, but how can it be in ours to submit to slavery?"

Athenian: "Because you would gain the advantage of submitting before suffering the *ultima ratio,* while we should profit by not having destroyed you."

Melian: "And an arrangement permitting us to remain at peace on friendly instead of hostile terms with you, but on a basis of neutrality, would not be acceptable to your Government?"

Athenian: "No—for we do not stand to suffer so much by your hostility as by the impression upon our subjects, who would take our friendship with you as a sign of our weakness and your hatred of us as a sign of your power."

Melian: "But are your subjects really so irrational that they place parties who have nothing to do with you in the same category as parties who are most of them your colonists and some of them conquered rebels?"

Athenian: "Yes, they do, because they consider that neither has a bad case in equity. For them, it is a question of strength on their side whether they maintain their independence, and of fear on ours whether we attack it; and, therefore, apart from the advantage of extending our Empire, you would minister to our security by being brought into subjection. The further fact that you are Islanders, and weaker brethren at that, renders it even more important for our security that you should not get the better of the masters of the sea."

Melian: "But do you not see security in another direction? (Here, again, we are forced to follow your lead in deposing us from the pedestal of Right and urging us to fall in with your interests, by explaining now in *our* turn where our own advantage lies and by attempting to prevail upon you if it happens to be identical with yours.) There are still the present neutrals to be considered, and how can you avoid bringing them into the war on the opposite side when they look at our fate and conclude that their turn will come to be attacked by you? If this is the case, you are simply intensifying the enemies whom you possess already and forcibly creating others who had never dreamed of intervention."

Athenian: "But it is not the case, because we do not see our chief danger in the continental peoples. The liberty which they enjoy may be relied upon to prevent them from taking measures against us in a hurry. It is the unsubjected Islanders, like yourselves, and the Islanders already exasperated by the pressure of our Empire, whom we chiefly have to fear. It is they who are most tempted to follow an irrational impulse which would involve both them and ourselves in unmistakable danger."

Melian: "But surely now, if you are prepared to take such fearful risks in order not to be deprived of your Empire, and if your enslaved peoples are prepared to do as much in order to escape your yoke, those of us who are still free would be cowards and weaklings indeed if we left any alternative untried before submitting to enslavement."

Athenian: "No, not if you are well advised, for it is not as if you had to contend with us on equal terms, with honor as the prize and disgrace as the penalty. The stakes are not honor but salvation, and the problem is to avoid resistance to an adversary who utterly outmatches you."

Melian: "Well, we are not unaware that in war the chances are occasionally more even than would be suggested by the relative size of the battalions. In our case, to yield is simply to abandon hope, while action will still preserve to us some hope of keeping our feet."

Athenian: "Hope? Why, what is Hope but Danger's comforter? Play her, perhaps, with a margin to lose on her, and at her worst she will not destroy you; but stake on her all that you possess (as this born spendthrift will tempt you to do), and you will see her in her true colors after the crash has come—then, and not till then, for, so long as there is still time to see through her and to beware, she is never found wanting. You, who are weak! You, whose fate will be settled by one turn of the scale! Do not be her victims and do not make the same mistake as all the others, who throw away the chances of survival that human means afford, and then when, in their extremity, their visible hopes desert them, address themselves to the invisible hopes of divination and oracles and all the other deceits which dangle the lure of Hope to bring men to destruction."

Melian: "You may be sure that we do not underestimate the difficulty of contending against the forces of Athens and the forces of Fortune when the scales are to be weighted against us. However, we trust the gods to see to it that Fortune does not tell against us, since Conscience is on our side and Right is not on yours; while, as to our inferiority of force, we trust to see that redressed by the military assistance of Lacedaemon, who cannot refuse to intervene, if only in response to the calls of kinship and honor. So our confidence is not so utterly irrational after all."

Athenian: "As to the favor of Heaven, we look forward to receiving our fair share of that ourselves. None of our demands and none of our actions trespass beyond the pale of human standards, whether for divine behavior or for mortal aspirations. We conjecture that Heaven, and we know for certain that mankind, is driven by a universal law of nature to rule wherever it is the stronger. This law was not of our making, nor have we been the first to act upon it when made. We found it in existence; we know that it will exist to all eternity after we are gone; and we act upon it now—well knowing, as we do so, that you and others would have done precisely the same had you possessed the same power as we. That is why, so far as Heaven is concerned, we neither fear nor have reason to fear that we shall find ourselves at a disadvantage; while as for your notion in regard to Lacedaemon —this astonishing belief that she will intervene on your behalf to preserve her honor—we congratulate you on your simplicity but do not envy your folly. The Lacedaemonians maintain admirably high standards in relation to themselves and their local institutions, but their behavior toward outsiders is —a very fruitful subject, which might perhaps be epitomized most expressively in the single statement that they identify Inclination with Honor and Interest with Right more blatantly than any other nation in the world—a mentality which hardly promises much for your present irrational hopes of salvation."

Melian: "Why, you have laid your finger upon the principal cause of our confidence in Lacedaemon, which we base upon her self-interest. Lacedaemon will never agree to lose the confidence of her friends in Hellas and to play into the hands of her enemies, as she must do if she betrays her colony of Melos."

Athenian: "Then you do not hold the view that Interest goes with security while Right and Honor are essentially perilous adventures—for which Lacedaemon usually displays singularly little alacrity?"

Melian: "Well, we believe at any rate that Lacedaemon would be less unwilling to embark upon these dangers on our behalf, and also that she would regard them as less risky in our case than in others. From the practical point of view we lie close off the Peloponnese, while from the psychological point of view we may be trusted to feel that blood is thicker than water."

Athenian: "Yes, but parties who are requested to give their military support do not look for their security to the good will evinced by the parties who ask the favor. They look, instead, for a decisive superiority of effective force, and no nation more so than the Lacedaemonians. Why, they distrust their national armaments so profoundly that it needs a whole host of allies to embolden them to attack their neighbors. Is it likely that they will venture across to an island while we command the sea?"

Melian: "But they might send substitutes, and the Cretan Sea is so wide that it is harder for the power commanding it to maintain her blockade than for blockade-runners to elude it. Besides, if this plan miscarried, they might still turn their attention to your territory and to the rest of your Allies who were not reached by Brasidas. In that case, you would have to fight for territory of your own and not for territory which does not belong to you."

Athenian: "These are hypotheses which it may be your turn soon to test by experience, though in fact you are well aware already that Athens has never in all her history abandoned a single siege for fear of a diversion. We are struck by the fact that, after professing your intention of guiding your country-men's feet into the way of salvation, you have talked at all this length without offering a single suggestion from which salvation could be expected with any confidence by reasonable human beings. Your strongest weapons are hopes yet unrealized, while the weapons in your hand are somewhat inadequate for holding out against the forces already arrayed against you. Indeed, you are showing yourselves irrational to a degree—unless you request us to retire and then arrive at some fresh and more sensible decision. We cannot conceive that you will take refuge in the illusion of Disgrace, which, in dangers that are disgraceful yet unmistakable, is the destroying angel of mankind. Often and often the victims, with eyes wide open to the tragedy into which they are rushing, are hypnotized by the magic of the fascinating word 'Disgrace' and pay for succumbing to a phrase by deliberately plunging into real and irremediable disasters—disasters which entail disgrace more disgraceful than any for being the concomitant of folly and not the consequence of Fortune. Against this snare you, if you are well advised, will be on your guard and will not feel it dishonorable to submit to moderate demands addressed to you by the greatest power in Hellas. After all, what do these demands amount to? That you should become tributary allies of Athens without forfeiting possession of your country; and that, when offered a choice between war and security, you should not obstinately insist upon choosing wrong. The three secrets of success are to hold your own against your equals, to keep on good terms with your superiors, and to treat your inferiors with consideration. Reconsider, we beg you, after we have withdrawn, and reflect again and yet again that you are taking a decision for your country —the only country that you possess, and a country whose fate hangs upon a single decision right or wrong."

Thereupon the Athenians withdrew from the conference; but the Melians, left to themselves, arrived at substantially the same views that they had expressed in reply to the Athenians, and announced them as follows: "Gentlemen, our views remain what they were at the beginning. We will not in a moment sign away the liberty of a country which has existed for seven hundred years. We put our trust in the Heaven-sent Fortune which has been our country's salvation hitherto, as well as in the earthly assistance which we expect from the Lacedaemonians, and we shall seek salvation herein. We make you the offer of a friendly neutrality on our part, conditional upon the withdrawal of your forces from our territory after the conclusion of a treaty upon terms acceptable to both of us."

After this announcement on the Melians' part, the Athenians broke the conference off with the following parting words: "Well, gentlemen, in our opinion your decisions reveal you as unique among mankind. You consider the future more certain than what stares you in the face; you behold the invisible an actuality with the eye of faith; you have blindly staked your uttermost upon Lacedaemon and Fortune and Hope, and utter will be your undoing."

The Athenian *parlementaires* now returned to the army, and the military commanders, finding the Melians obdurate, immediately started operations. Dividing the sectors among the contingents, they drew lines all round the town, in which they subsequently left a naval and military garrison including national as well as Allied troops, while the major part of the force went home. The force left at Melos stayed on and maintained the siege . . . and during the same season the Athenian garrison at Pylos captured a vast amount of plunder from the Lacedaemonians; but even this did not bring Lacedaemon to the point of denouncing the peace and declaring war upon Athens. She merely authorized her citizens by proclamation to privateer against Athenian citizens. . . . The Melians, for their part, captured the sector of the Athenian lines opposite the *piazza* by a night attack, in which they inflicted casualties and brought in foodstuffs and as many other supplies as possible before withdrawal. Thereafter they remained on the defensive, while the Athenians reorganized their sentry system —and so the summer ended.

Next winter, the Lacedaemonians were on the verge of invading the territory of Argos when the frontier ritual [1] miscarried, whereupon they went home again. The Argives were so much encouraged by the Lacedaemonians' hesitation that

---

[1] When a Hellenic army crossed the frontier, the diviners sacrificed an animal and predicted, by an inspection of the offal, whether the campaign would be a success. [ED.]

they arrested a number of suspect residents.[1] At about the same date, the Melians again captured a sector of the Athenian lines at a different point where the garrison was in weak force. This incident provoked the dispatch of reinforcements from Athens under the command of Philocrates, son of Dēmeas. The siege was now pressed with vigor, there were symptoms of treachery within the walls, and the result was that Melos surrendered at discretion. The Athenians used their discretion to put to death all Melian prisoners of military age and to sell the women and children into slavery. They afterward colonized the place themselves with five hundred Athenian settlers.

.   .   .   .   .   .

The same winter, the Athenians proposed to send a fresh overseas expedition to Sicily on a greater scale than the previous expedition under Laches and Eurymedon. Their objective was nothing less than the conquest of the island, for most people at Athens had no practical knowledge of the size of Sicily, of the total numbers of the Hellenic and non-Hellenic population, or of the fact that they were embarking upon a war of hardly inferior dimensions to their war against the Peloponnesian Confederacy. . . .[2]

THE PEACE DEBATE AT NAUPACTUS
(217 B.C.) [3]
(POLYBIUS: Book V, chapters 103–105)

WHEN King Philip had been joined at Panormus[4] by the delegates of his Allies, he sent off Aratus and Taurion with some of their colleagues to see the Aetolians. These emissaries found the Aetolians assembled in full session at Naupactus, and, after a short conversation, which revealed the Aetolians' anxiety for a settlement, they sailed back again to Philip in order to enlighten him on the situation. The Aetolians, in their eagerness to end the war, sent off with them emissaries of their own to Philip, with an invitation to ferry his army over into their territory, expressing the hope that a discussion at

[1] Some of the persons marked down for arrest managed to slip through their fingers. [AUTHOR.]
[2] The story of the Athenian disaster in Sicily follows. [ED.]
[3] Since 219 B.C., a desultory war had been in progress between the Aetolian Confederacy on the one hand and King Philip V of Macedonia with his Achaean, Boeotian, Acarnanian, and Epirot Allies on the other. [ED.]
[4] A Peloponnesian harbor facing the town of Naupactus (across the Gulf of Corinth). [AUTHOR.]

close quarters might bring things to a satisfactory issue. The King was influenced by this invitation to sail across to the "Hollows of Naupactia," [1] where he pitched his camp, drew a fortified line round his ships as well as his land forces, and waited patiently for the moment of meeting. The Aetolians presented themselves (unarmed) en masse, halted about 400 yards from Philip's army, and made overtures for discussing the points at issue. The King's first step was to send off all the representatives of the Allies with instructions to offer peace to the Aetolians on terms of *uti possidetis*. The Aetolians accepted this offer with alacrity, and from that point onward the discussion of the details was conducted by a constant interchange of emissaries. The majority of these conversations I propose to omit, since they contain nothing worthy of record, but I shall record the speech addressed, at the first meeting, by Agelāus of Naupactus to the King and his Allies there present.

The ideal, said Agelaus, was that Hellenes should never go to war with one another at all. They should be profoundly thankful to the gods if they succeeded, by maintaining absolute unanimity and by linking hands like people crossing rivers, in flinging back the onslaughts of the non-Hellenic world for the common salvation of their countries and themselves. If this were a counsel of perfection, he did at any rate plead for harmony and watchfulness at the actual moment, when they saw before their eyes the scale on which the war in the West was being fought and the massiveness of the forces engaged in it. It was evident already to anybody who took the slightest interest in public affairs that, whether the Carthaginians were victorious over the Romans or the Romans over the Carthaginians, there was no probability whatever of the victors remaining content with their dominion over the Hellenes of Italy and Sicily. No, the victors would come to Hellas, would extend their enterprises and would spread their forces beyond their proper limits. Therefore the speaker begged all his hearers to be watchful in this crisis, King Philip above all. How should the King keep watch? By abandoning his destructive warfare against Hellas which was rendering her an easy prey for the aggressor, reversing his policy, and consulting her interests as if she were flesh of his flesh. Let him make it his rule to promote the welfare of every part of Hellas as if it were his own intimate possession. This was the policy to make the Hellenes not only his friends but his steadfast companions in arms against foreign attack, and to make outsiders less inclined to plot the overthrow of his power under the overwhelming impression of the confidence which

[1] A locality about 2½ miles distant from the town of Naupactus itself. [AUTHOR.]

Hellas reposed in him. If the King thirsted for action, the speaker begged him to look toward the West and to direct his attention to the war in progress in Italy. If he played a waiting hand with judgment, he might aspire, when the moment came, to world power—an ambition to which the present crisis was not unfavorable. As regarded his quarrels with the Hellenes and the wars in which he pursued them, he implored the King to postpone them until the interludes, and to concentrate his efforts upon the limited object of preserving a free hand to make peace or war with his Hellenic neighbors at his pleasure. If once the clouds now appearing above the Western horizon were allowed by the King to advance until they overhung the longitude of Hellas, "I am in deadly apprehension," concluded the speaker, "that the truces and the wars and all this childish nonsense in which we now indulge with one another may, in the event, be so drastically knocked out of all of us that we shall beseech the gods to restore to us this precious freedom to make war and peace with one another at our pleasure or, in other words, to settle our family quarrels among ourselves."

This speech from Agelaus influenced all the Allies in the direction of making peace, and particularly Philip, in whose mind Agelaus's words exactly harmonized with the inclination already implanted there by the suggestions of Demetrius.[1] Accordingly the parties came to an agreement with one another over the points of detail, ratified the treaty, and then separated in order to bear home to their respective countries the blessing of peace in place of war.

[1] Demetrius of Pharus (the island in the Dalmatian Archipelago which is now called Lesina) had been expelled from his principality for piracy by the Romans in 219 B.C. and had been given asylum at the court of Macedonia. [ED.]

FINIS

INDEX

MENTOR Books on the Ancient World

THE SATYRICON
by Petronius translated by William Arrowsmith.
A classic recreation of Nero's pleasure-loving Rome by the cultured cynic, Petronius, in a brilliant new translation.
(#MT716—75¢)

THE METAMORPHOSES *by Ovid translated by Horace Gregory.*
Ovid's magnificent collection of legends and myths, translated into vital modern poetry. (#MY792—$1.25)

THE OEDIPUS PLAYS OF SOPHOCLES *translated by Paul Roche.*
A dramatic new verse translation of "Oedipus the King," "Oedipus at Colonus," and "Antigone," suitable for acting as well as reading. (#MQ807—95¢)

THREE GREAT PLAYS OF EURIPIDES *translated by Rex Warner.*
The tragedies of "Medea," "Hippolytus," and "Helen," in a new translation by Rex Warner, classicist and author of "The Young Caesar." (#MT241—75¢)

GREAT DIALOGUES OF PLATO *translated by W. H. D. Rouse.*
A new translation into direct, forceful modern English of "The Republic" and other dialogues of the great philosopher of ancient Greece. (#MQ672—95¢)

WAR COMMENTARIES OF CAESAR *translated by Rex Warner.*
Julius Caesar's classic first-hand account of his military campaigns in an outstanding translation by the author of *The Young Caesar.* (#MQ802—95¢)

THE ILIAD OF HOMER *translated by W. H. D. Rouse.*
A forceful prose translation of Homer's great epic of the Trojan War, by a noted English scholar. (#MT650—75¢)

THE ODYSSEY OF HOMER *translated by W. H. D. Rouse.*
A modern prose translation of the world's greatest adventure story, the travels of Ulysses. (#MT677—75¢)

THE GREEK PHILOSOPHERS *by Rex Warner.*
The basic writings of philosophers from Thales to Plotinus, with commentary by the editor, a distinguished classical scholar. (#MT759—75¢)

The Mentor Philosophers

The entire range of Western speculative thinking from the Middle Ages to modern times is presented in this series of six volumes. "A very important and interesting series."—*Gilbert Highet*

THE AGE OF BELIEF: The Medieval Philosophers
   edited by Anne Fremantle   (#MQ739—95¢)
   "Highly commendable . . . provides an excellent beginning volume."   —*The Classical Bulletin*

THE AGE OF ADVENTURE: The Renaissance Philosophers
   edited by Giorgio de Santillana.   (#MT437—75¢)
   "The most exciting and varied in the series."
                                        —*New York Times*

THE AGE OF REASON: The 17th Century Philosophers
   edited by Stuart Hampshire.   (#MQ833—95¢)
   "His (Hampshire's) book is a most satisfactory addition to an excellent series."   —*Saturday Review*

THE AGE OF ENLIGHTENMENT: The 18th Century Philosophers *edited by Sir Isaiah Berlin.*   (#MQ689—95¢)
   "(Sir Isaiah) has one of the liveliest and most stimulating minds among contemporary philosophers."
                                        —*N. Y. Herald Tribune*

THE AGE OF IDEOLOGY: The 19th Century Philosophers
   edited by Henry D. Aiken.   (#MQ733—95¢)
   ". . . perhaps the most distinct intellectual contribution made in the series."   —*New York Times*

THE AGE OF ANALYSIS: 20th Century Philosophers
   edited by Morton White.   (#MQ786—95¢)
   "No other book remotely rivals this as the best available introduction to 20th century philosophy."
                                        —*N. Y. Herald Tribune*

TO OUR READERS: If your dealer does not have the SIGNET and MENTOR books you want, you may order them by mail enclosing the list price plus 10¢ a copy to cover mailing. (New York City residents add 5% Sales Tax. Other New York State residents add 2% plus any local sales or use taxes.) Please order books by book number and title. If you would like our free catalog, please request it by postcard only. The New American Library, Inc., P. O. Box 1478, Church St. Station, New York, N.Y. 10008.